Solving
EEO Problems

A Guide to EEO

Law and Practice

Executive Enterprises Publications Co., Inc.

CONTENTS

CONTENTS

CASE STUDIES

INTRODUCTION

Equal employment opportunity is a fact of life for today's employers—but not an easy fact of life.

Laws, regulations, court decisions, and employee complaints make the employer's life a maze of confusion and regulatory obfuscation, obstacles and dangers, challenges and rewards. Businesses need the best professional and legal advice available to lead them through the labyrinth of EEO problems; and this collection of twenty-five articles culled from the quarterly journal EEO TODAY is designed to do just that. The articles inform, clarify, analyze, suggest, recommend, and warn, providing the type of nuts-and-bolts advice that will help managers meet their increasing responsibilities to their employees and to their organization's goals in this EEO era.

The EEO field is developing rapidly, and these articles, written over a period of four years, reflect developments as they occurred. In the rare instances where events may have outstripped portions of the material, the reader has been alerted.

In addition to being *difficult*, EEO is also a comparatively *new* fact of life. EEO was born sixteen years ago with Title VII of the Civil Rights Act of 1964, which barred employment discrimination based on race, color, religion, national origin, and, almost as an afterthought, sex. Protection grew through the sixties and seventies so that the handicapped, Vietnam-era veterans, pregnant women, and workers up to age 70 have been added to the roster of those groups falling under the expanding area of government protection.

New concepts, new terminology, new responsibilities have been added to the field—and the employer must be on top of it all. For example:

- *Equal pay for equal work*, the basis for the Equal Pay Act of 1963, is evolving into the demand of *equal pay for jobs of com-*

parable worth—increasingly a rallying cry for women who argue that pay differences between dissimilar jobs are rooted in sex discrimination.

- The Equal Employment Opportunity Commission has mounted an attack on *"systemic discrimination,"* establishing a separate office within the agency to deal with institutionalized employment practices that hinder job opportunities for women and minorities.

- In the aftermath of government-required affirmative action programs to advance the opportunities of discriminated-against groups came the cry of *"reverse discrimination"* by white males who challenged the policy in courts, resulting in the landmark *Bakke* and *Weber* Supreme Court decisions; these rulings, while answering some questions, left many others unresolved. The tightrope between preferential affirmative action for minorities and women and equal opportunities for each individual, as one of our authors point out, can be precarious indeed.

- *Sexual harassment* on the job, *uniform selection guidelines*, new methods of *selection validation*, the *networking* approach to finding qualified females and minority managers, discrimination-free *employee benefit plans*—all are new and complex issues that employers *must* understand to cope with the realities of the 1980s.

While the problems associated with these EEO issues are difficult, the rewards of solving them are high: a motivated work force that will perform with renewed vigor to advance the objectives of the organization. An equitable and rational EEO policy will result in the most effective utilization of human resources—the backbone of any successful organization.

EEOC's New Thrust: An Attack on Systemic Discrimination

When Eleanor Holmes Norton took over the U.S. Equal Employment Opportunity Commission in June 1977, one of her primary goals was to mount a "systemic attack" on job discrimination. Thus, in addition to revamping the Commission's organizational structure and creating new systems for the processing of individual complaints, Norton established an Office of Systemic Programs, designed to combat institutionalized employment practices that restrict job opportunities for minorities and women.

The Office of Systemic Programs includes a headquarters office in Washington, D.C., and separate systemic units in each of EEOC's twenty-two district offices throughout the country. A systemic inquiry begins with a review of the employer's work force statistics and other relevant data, followed by selection of targets for further investigation. A systemic charge is issued by a member of the Commission and does not require a formal complaint from an individual or group of employees.

Voluntary compliance is the aim of the systemic program. At all stages of the process, EEOC says it will be prepared to settle with respondents who agree to end past discrimination, take affirmative action to prevent future discrimination, and provide appropriate compensation for identifiable victims of discrimination.

To provide its readers with a clearer understanding of EEOC's systemic program and to keep track of new developments and future plans, EEO TODAY put a series of questions to *Michael Middleton*, long-time Title VII lawyer, who is the new director of EEOC's Office of Systemic Programs.

Research, investigation, and litigation form the procedural framework for the systemic program. Could you explain the process for a systemic charge and how these three steps relate?

The Office of Systemic Programs is separated into three divisions—research or technical services, investigative and enforcement.

Basically, the investigators design and carry out the investigation, delving into data on applicants, hires, promotions, wages, and so on, and also into the employment system itself—the company's standards, qualifications, and processes. The investigators draft the decision, define the scope of relief from the remedial programs, and then negotiate the package with the employer.

The litigation/enforcement division is, of course, the "stick." Once a case, which has gone through the administrative process, reaches a point where conciliation attempts are unsuccessful, the case goes to this division for enforcement. Of course, lawyers in that division serve in an advisory capacity throughout the investigation process.

The technical services division is composed of psychologists, statisticians, and other technical people who assist in the investigations. For instance, labor market analysis, review of test validation, tests of statistical significance—these are all done by the technical services division. The division also assists district offices in selecting targets for investigation. The responsibility of this division is to analyze available data and, through scientific methods, to determine which employers in each geographic area are most likely to have discriminatory practices. These employers, therefore, would be appropriate for a Commissioner's charge.

Much of the published material on the systemic program says that the Commission will use statistics and "other information" in selecting systemic targets. What is actually included in this "other information"?

Clearly, EEO-1 data (Employer Information Report) is the underpinning of that targeting process. But this data must be compared to something. We will be using Census Bureau data, demographic data, and work force statistics. In addition, we can use data collected by the Office of Federal Contract Compliance Programs—compliance reviews produce a great deal of data on employers who also come under EEOC's jurisdiction. Individual case investigations, too, generally produce data which can be useful to us in a systemic case.

And occassionally, we receive a petition from a private organization—for example, a local community group, the Inc. Fund,
the Lawyers Committee. These petitions sometimes provide data and
sources of information that the group has uncovered through its own
investigations. Then, it becomes a matter of pulling together everything available to us and using all the information to make our determination whether to recommend a charge.

Once the headquarters staff has completed what it can do with the
materials here, we send the names of potential targets to the district
offices. The district offices then conduct further local research and select those potential targets they think most appropriate. The knowledge of the district office staff regarding the local situation is essential
to any proper evaluation of a target.

**How you will actually identify and select subjects for systemic inves-
tigation?**

As I mentioned, selection of the actual targets is done by the district offices. They then prepare a presentation memorandum and submit that document to headquarters for approval. We (the Headquarters Office of Systemic Programs) then determine whether their
selection was appropriate and whether it fits into the program
guidelines. If the presentation memo is acceptable and shows promise, it is then submitted to a Commissioner for the issuance of a
Commissioner's charge. At that point, a full-scale investigation is begun.

**What is the relationship between headquarters and the field after
the charge is issued?**

After a Commissioner's charge is issued, it is sent to the field. The
district office does the actual "hands-on" investigation. But the investigation is tracked, in a sense, by headquarters. We will check time
frames for an investigation, for example—the whole management-by-
objectives system goes into the process.

The Office of Systemic Programs has an auditing function. We have
designed the program—the investigation methods and standards—and
we are responsible for seeing that they are maintained. Of course, if
the district offices need technical assistance—labor market analysis,
work force data, statistical analysis, test validation, and so on—these
questions can and should be forwarded to headquarters.

Finally, we are the conduit to the Commission for final actions
—only the Office of Systemic Programs can recommend issuance of a

charge or a decision, so we are directly accountable for the quality of the work and its adherence to the program defined by the Commission.

Legal assistance in those investigations is generally given by the regional attorney's office, under the professional supervision of the General Counsel's office here. Thus, systemic charge processing is a joint effort between the investigative and legal arms, with most of the functions carried out by the district offices.

Currently, we have twenty-two systemic units in our district offices. Washington headquarters also has a systemic unit. At the moment, that unit is working on existing cases inherited from the old organization. Eventually, however, there will be a headquarters systemic program that will function much like the field units, the difference being that the headquarters systemic unit will concentrate on cases that are national in scope, cases involving employers with facilities in several districts or major national corporations that we believe could be more appropriately handled within headquarters.

Staff in the district offices received training before the systemic program was undertaken. Can you describe the components of the training program?

Each investigator received five days of training; 125 persons were trained. Basically, the program was a walk-through of an actual investigation. Trainees were taken step by step through the whole investigative process. We had interviewing techniques; sessions on how to deal with various types of respondent behavior; what kind of information to elicit and how to arrange, analyze, and interpret it; how to document the existence of discrimination and how to pin down its source and effect—all basic investigative techniques.

The idea was to centralize the training because the methodology is now uniform. Everyone in the country had the same training and will handle the cases in similar fashion. We have taken great pains to design an investigative approach that meets our needs but is not burdensome to employers. We want to do our work well and make it possible for employers to cooperate. We want to finish our cases in a short time—comparatively speaking—and get on to the next case.

What is Early Litigation Identification (ELI)? How does it differ from and relate to the overall systemic program?

The ELI program is designed to take care of a problem we recognized when we set up the systemic program. The systemic program allows the Commission to select the major cases it wishes to investigate, rather than respond solely to charges filed by others. However, we still want to respond to meritorious complaints of class discrimination that come to us under the normal charge-processing systems. Many people have said that such complaints have been ignored as a result of rapid charge processing and the revamping of Commission procedures for dealing with charges. The ELI system is a mechanism to identify those cases that may have good potential as class cases. Cases identified under the ELI program will get special treatment, the kind of systemic approach that other cases, not identified under ELI, will not get.

The rapid charge-processing system was designed to deal expeditiously, yet fairly, with individual complaints. In the past, all broad charges were handled broadly; as a result, Commission resources were expended—indeed, exhausted—on cases that often were undeserving of such treatment. When rapid charge processing was developed, the fear was that the Commission "threw the baby out with the bath water"—quickly resolving charges that might otherwise be potential systemic vehicles. ELI is designed to "save the baby."

As initially designed, the systemic program was to be based largely on statistical evidence. Since more and more companies are attempting to develop statistical evidence of legitimate, non-discriminatory reasons for apparent adverse impact, do you think a statistical approach can be effective? If not—or at least, not by itself—what approach do you think can bring the Commission's desired results?

Back in the "old days," it was very easy to look at a company's profile, compare it with the local work force figures of minorities and women, show a disparity, and run to court, saying, "There is discrimination here," unless the employer can prove the contrary. In those days, employers were not really familiar with Title VII law, and they had not developed the capability to respond effectively to those kinds of allegations. The courts, on the other hand, were very excited about Title VII law. All this was back in the sixties, when civil rights was on everybody's mind. The federal enforcement agencies were very involved, defining the problems and designing remedies.

The tone of the country has changed; the mood has changed. Many people feel that minorities have made enough gains over the past ten or fifteen years. Moreover, industry has decided that Title VII is here to stay; and they recognize the need to develop a capability to respond to Title VII charges.

There was a time when the defendant would come into court with

13

a statistician who would run circles around the plaintiff's statisticians. They would quickly show that, although there was a disparity, it was due to nondiscriminatory factors. Our program will now go through that stage in the investigation, before a determination is issued.

I think statistics can work in the systemic program. Not statistics alone, of course—statistics have, in fact, never made cases. Statistics show a problem. Or they indicate the possibility of a problem. But in order to make a case, those practices that may be discriminatory must be identified. In this connection, you have to deal with the non-discriminatory reasons the employer offers to explain those statistical patterns. When a prima facie case has been established with statistics and the employer has provided data supporting his defenses, we have to be sophisticated enough to respond to those defenses. We must go beyond the basic statistical disparity and get into the reasons for the disparity, finding actual examples of how a given practice affects people.

When I was trying Title VII cases (at the Justice Department and the Lawyers Committee for Civil Rights Under Law), I never went into court with statistics alone. What you do is this: First, you learn how the company works. You learn as much about their personnel procedures as the personnel director knows. Then you look at the statistics to see where people may be affected adversely. Then you attempt to determine the reasons for this adverse impact. If, in fact, the exclusionary standard is job-related, necessary to the performance of that particular job, it is not illegal discrimination.

Even when you establish statistically that a practice has an exclusionary impact and it is not job-related, it is always helpful to present the employer or the court with people who have been adversely affected by the practice. It is probably not legally necessary to do so, but it is certainly impressive. For example, if a test is the exclusionary practice you are dealing with and you are able to find capable people excluded from the job solely because of the examination, it impresses the judge. It impresses a company president when you bring him blacks or women or Hispanics who've done a good job for the company for ten years, who have been trying to move up for ten years but have failed to do so because they couldn't pass a certain test. You go to the employer and say, "Here are good, loyal employees who can do the work, who know the company, but who can't get the job because they can't pass the test. And you have not been able to show me that this test is really necessary."

Walking into an executive's office ready to fight makes no sense. Rather, an investigator should go to the employer and say, "We have some statistics here which show that you may have a problem in your personnel practices. We'd like to look at some of your files. We'd like to study your personnel practices and see what may be causing the problems—if, indeed, such a problem exists." Employers should be addressed in a logical, pleasant way.

Once a decision has been issued and conciliation is in process, the Commission is saying this: "These are the problems; this is what we see. This practice is not really necessary to job performance and it has adverse impact, which is against the law. If you change this, your whole operation will run more smoothly. You will increase morale. Everything will work much better and people who are protected by the law will be assured of their rights."

I think the idea of voluntary compliance can work. And we won't get people to volunteer by beating them with statistics and acting tough. We can achieve voluntary compliance by dealing in a businesslike way with business people.

I may be naive, but that seems to be a fairly simple concept. Of course, we need some strong litigation in our back pocket. Part of the reason for merging the legal and investigative functions of the systemic program is to assure that the litigators are involved in the whole process from the beginning. That way, if negotiations break down, we can move quickly into an enforcement posture.

Title VII law is becoming very interesting. Today, it is very sophisticated, very technical. That discrimination still exists is a fact. The problem becomes proving that it's there. I think, with the kind of expertise we are developing here, we will be able to do that.

How many systemic inquiries do you estimate the Commission would undertake over a year? Of these, how many do you think will lead to a finding of discrimination?

The way we have designed the program, ideally almost all systemic charges will result in findings of discrimination. And, we hope, they will all result in a conciliation agreement or a consent decree. This is because, hopefully, our targeting process is sophisticated enough to identify, at the outset, those companies with the problems.

How many systemic charges will we be able to process a year? That is difficult to say. I would hope that each of the twenty-two systemic units would do five or six systemic cases a year, which would mean approximately 150 Commissioner's charges issued in a year.

Commissioner Norton has stated that settlement is the goal of the systemic program. Given the current atmosphere, do you think em-

ployers will want to settle or do you think they may litigate aggressively? Do you have any prediction on what percentage of the charges will be successfully conciliated and what percentage will be litigated?

Some employers are very eager to do the right thing. They develop meaningful affirmative action programs; they do an effective job of recruiting minorities and females. Other employers will fight tooth and nail. They simply do not want any federal involvement in their business, particularly any federal civil rights involvement.

Then, there is a large group of employers in the middle. They think, for the most part, they're doing the right thing. But they probably know they have some problems. They are concerned about the time and expense of litigation. They compare the cost of litigation to the cost of conciliation and then determine the route they will take. They would probably litigate if they thought we were an incompetent organization, that it would take years for the case to go to court, giving them time to improve their minority participation and increase their chances of winning the case.

An employer's willingness to settle, then, is very much dependent on EEOC's ability to produce good, well-reasoned, well-conceived, logical investigations and findings. The moment we start doing that consistently, employers are very likely to go along with us.

Settlement is a meeting of the minds, an agreement on what the problems are and what the solution is. If we go to the employer with a well-conceived notion of the problem and the remedy, I don't see any logical alternative for the employer but settlement.

Now, there may be those interested in fighting for the sake of fighting. But I certainly don't know many employers interested in setting legal precedents. Most employers simply want to get on with their business, with as little federal involvement as possible.

If we can show employers how they are violating the law, how they can remedy that situation and avoid the time and expense of litigation, and if we come to them with some reason, logic, and professionalism, I think Commissioner Norton's desire for settlements will be achieved.

Settlement often has many advantages over the results of litigation, because frequently, courts and lawyers, in the heat of litigation, don't reach the best solutions. On the other hand, when a company agrees to a plan, they are more likely to cooperate in carrying out that plan. Indeed, Title VII was designed by Congress with voluntary compliance as its primary goal. It makes sense for us to carry out Title VII in the way Congress intended.

What do you envision will be the employer response to the systemic program?

Many employers seem curious about the program. They want to know more about the standards for selecting targets and so on. They are quite excited about this new, logical approach. I hope to get that tone across to anyone I deal with. We will *not* come into people's offices, banging on their desks, demanding some outrageous remedy. But we do intend to get effective remedies, remedies to what we see as the problem. That is what the Office of Systemic Programs is all about.

LAW

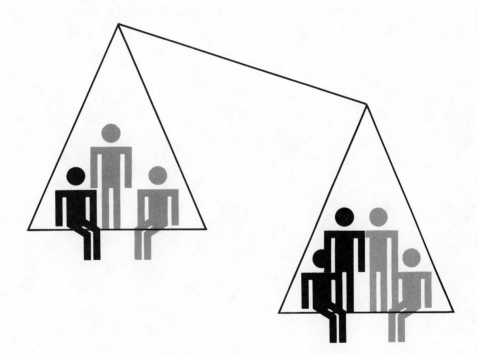

Federal Laws
Barring Discrimination
against the Handicapped:
An Overview

Michael A. Hood

The next "explosion" in EEO law will be in the area of discrimination against the handicapped. Already, significant cases concerning the federal laws that protect the handicapped against discrimination are winding their way through the lower federal courts. Some have even reached the Supreme Court. In addition, no fewer than thirty-eight states, plus the District of Columbia, have enacted their own laws affording varying degrees of protection to the physically and/or mentally handicapped.

This explosion may ultimately reach *all* employers, but for now, federal contractors are the most immediately affected.[1] The federal laws that forbid discrimination against the handicapped presently apply only to employers who are government contractors or receive federal financial assistance.

These laws have a broader sweep even than Title VII, the Age Discrimination in Employment Act, and Executive Order 11246 and Revised Order No. 4. Indeed, federal law[2] defines the term

---

Michael A. Hood is with the Newport Beach office of the Los Angeles law firm of Paul, Hastings, Janofsky & Walker.

21

"handicapped individual" so broadly that almost everyone—black, white, male, female—at some time in his or her life will qualify for the protection of federal law. The Office of Federal Contract Compliance Programs (OFCCP), which administers the federal law as it applies to federal government contractors, seems intent on stretching the law to prohibit discrimination based not just on handicap but on *any physical condition*.

The federal law that affects government contractors is section 503 of the Rehabilitation Act of 1973. That section prohibits federal contractors (with $2,500 or more in government contracts) from discriminating against employees and prospective employees because of their physical or mental handicaps. It also requires them to take affirmative action to employ and advance in employment qualified handicapped individuals.

Who is "Handicapped" under the Rehabilitation Act ?

The Rehabilitation Act defines a "handicapped" individual as one who:

(A) has a physical or mental impairment which *substantially limits* one or more of such person's *major life activities*,

(B) has a *record* of such an impairment, or

(C) is *regarded* as having such an impairment. [Emphasis added.]

However, the Office of Federal Contract Compliance Programs (OFCCP), which administers the Act, has issued regulations that greatly expand the definition.[3] The OFCCP regulations define "substantially limit" as referring to those impairments that make their sufferers experience difficulty in securing, retaining, or advancing in employment. Moreover, according to the OFCCP regulations, "major life activities" include such activities as communication, walking, self-care, vocational training, transportation, education, and *employment*. In the case of *OFCCP v. E. E. Black, Ltd.*, (discussed in more detail below), the OFCCP even *further* broadened the statutory definition of "handicapped" by defining the term "impairment" to mean any condition that weakens, diminishes, or otherwise damages an individual's health or mental or physical activities.

Subpart (B) includes in the broad definition of "handicapped" those individuals who may have once had but are now free from a physical or mental handicap, or those who were or are erroneously classified as handicapped. Subpart (C) includes those individuals whose mental or physical impairments do not in fact substantially limit their major life activities, but who are *perceived* by others to be limited by their disabilities.

Thus, the term "handicapped" as used in the Act can cover a vast multitude of people—such as those with heart conditions, congenital back problems, epilepsy, terminal cancer, allergies, even alcoholism and drug addiction. Indeed, because the OFCCP regulations define "handicap" exclusively in terms of employment, the list of potential employees covered by the Act extends virtually to anyone who has or has had a physical or mental condition that an employer takes or has taken into consideration in making an employment decision.

What Are a Government Contractor's Obligations under the Act?

1. The Obligation Not to Discriminate

By entering into a government contract, a federal contractor agrees not to discriminate, on the basis of a physical or mental handicap, against any employee, or prospective employee, in regard to any position for which the individual is *qualified*. An individual is deemed *qualified* for a position if he or she is capable of performing it with "reasonable accommodation" by the employer to the physical or mental impairment. A reasonable accommodation is one that imposes no undue hardship on the conduct of a contractor's business. In determining whether a hardship is undue, a contractor may consider its costs, the resultant impact of an accommodation on safety, and the contractor's business necessity for *not* making the accommodation.[4] The concept can best be understood by considering a few examples.

For instance, consider a nearly deaf person who applies for a job as PBX operator/receptionist. Obviously, such a person is not qualified for that job. But let us assume that a mechanical device can be attached to a telephone to enable the individual to hear and speak. If that device cost only $25, an employer would probably be required to offer the job to the nearly deaf person and to make the accommodation of purchasing the equipment. On the other hand, if the device cost $25,000, the employer likely would not have to do so. In the latter case, the *cost* of the accommodation to the person's handicap would make it unreasonable to require the contractor to purchase it.

Or consider a person who is confined to a wheelchair and who applies for a job on an assembly line. Assume also that that person can perform all of the movements necessary to the job except one, which requires the machine operator to be able to stand up. Strictly speaking, that applicant is not qualified for the job, because he or she cannot perform all of the duties of the position. Assume also, however, that it could be arranged for another employee to perform that one movement. If that arrangement would slow production only slightly, the employer would probably be required to offer the job to the wheelchair applicant, and accommodate the individual by restructuring the job so that responsibility for the performance of that one motion is shifted to the other employee. If that arrangement, however, slowed production substantially, say 25 percent, the employer would probably not be obligated to make the accommodation. In the latter case, the employer's business necessity would excuse it from making the accommodation.

To date, the single most common problem that government contractors have experienced in terms of their obligation not to discriminate has been with applicants who have physical conditions (especially back problems or heart conditions) that make hiring them risky for both the contractor and the applicants themselves because their performance of work is likely to cause further deterioration of their conditions. Most employers have traditionally declined to hire an applicant whose physical condition might be adversely affected by performing the duties of the job. The OFCCP's position, however, is that an employer may consider only an employee's *present ability* to perform the job. An employer cannot refuse to hire an applicant solely because his or her physical condition is likely to be aggravated, even if irreparably, if the individual performs the duties of the job for any length of time.

This was the central issue in the first reported decision out of the OFCCP in the handicap area, *OFCCP v. E. E. Black, Ltd.*[5] In that case, the employer declined to hire an individual whose pre-employment back x-ray revealed a congenital back defect, which the company doctor concluded rendered him a "poor risk" for heavy labor. At the trial, expert testimony from one doctor established there was a 75-80 percent chance that the employee would suffer back problems in the future if he continued to perform heavy labor such as he had applied for. Nonetheless, the OFCCP ruled that the employer had violated the Act. Concern about the *future* effects of job performance on the applicant's health are not relevant. According to the decision, all that matters is *present* ability to do the job.[6]

This OFCCP position is extreme, and may not be upheld in the courts. Many *state* courts, interpreting state handicap discrimination laws, have concluded that an employer legitimately *may* refuse to hire someone with a handicap if performance of the duties of the job would likely aggravate or accelerate the rate of degeneration of the individual's physical condition. Unless and until the OFCCP's position is reversed, however, a government contractor who makes an employment decision based on concern about the future effects of employment on an individual's physical condition risks a violation of the Rehabilitation Act.

2. The Obligation to Take Affirmative Action to Employ and Advance the Handicapped

Government contractors are required to take "affirmative action" to employ and advance in employment qualified handicapped persons. The OFCCP's regulations set forth the actions a contractor must take to achieve affirmative action. The emphasis of those regulations is on identification of handicapped workers currently in the contractor's work force, coupled with efforts by the contractor to increase the flow of handicapped applicants. Affirmative action in the handicapped area includes the following:

First, affirmative action includes posting notices. The OFCCP regulations require a contractor to post in conspicuous places throughout its premises notices that describe its duty to take affirmative action on behalf of the handicapped, and notices that inform employees and applicants of their rights under the Rehabilitation Act.

Second, contractors must review their personnel policies to determine whether they provide for careful consideration of handicapped applicants and employees for vacancies filled by hiring or promotion and for training opportunities. In its regulations, the OFCCP stresses that a contractor may find it necessary to modify its personnel procedures to give handicapped individuals the proper consideration, and it has a suggested procedure that requires a contractor to segregate the applications of handicapped individuals and note on them any relevant actions it takes—positions for which it considers them, promotions offered to them, accommodations made for them, etc.

Third, a contractor is required to review all its physical and mental job qualification requirements to make sure that, if they tend to screen out qualified handicapped persons, they are job-related, and are consistent with business necessity and safe performance on the job. To the extent they are not, they must be modified or eliminated.

For example, it would be inappropriate for a contractor to have a heavy lifting requirement for a clerical job, or a policy of hiring only high school graduates or persons of a certain I.Q. for very menial labor.

Fourth, a contractor must make "reasonable accommodation" to the physical and mental impairments of applicants and employees. This requirement is merely a restatement of the contractor's obligation not to discriminate against "qualified handicapped persons," i.e., those that can perform a given job with the aid of reasonable accommodation to their handicap.

Fifth, a contractor cannot pay or offer to pay any handicapped employee or applicant less than a nonhandicapped employee or applicant merely because he or she receives disability income, pension income, or some other benefit from a collateral source.

Sixth, a contractor must actively recruit handicapped persons for both entry level positions and promotions. The OFCCP recognizes that the scope of recruitment efforts will vary with the contractor's size and resources and the extent to which its existing practices are already adequate. Obviously, the bigger the company, the more will be required. The OFCCP has suggested some recruitment steps to take in seeking qualified handicapped persons:

(1) The contractor should develop internal checks to insure that its affirmative action program is fully implemented.

(2) The contractor should consider seeking help from recruiting sources, including state employment security agencies, state vocational rehabilitation agencies, college placement offices, state education agencies, labor organizations, and other organizations for the handicapped, to help meet its goals of hiring and advancing handicapped persons.

(3) The contractor should consider recruiting applicants from educational institutes that have training programs for the handicapped, such as schools for the blind, deaf, or retarded.

(4) The contractor should consider contacting social services agencies, organizations for the handicapped, and vocational rehabilitation agencies to seek advice and assistance in the placement, recruitment, and training of qualified handicapped persons, plus the making of reasonable accommodations for them.

(5) The contractor should review its employment records to learn whether there are in its work force promotable handicapped individuals, and should further evaluate whether it is fully using or developing their skills.

(6) The contractor should include handicapped workers whenever it uses pictures of employees in any type of promotional or help-wanted advertising.

(7) The contractor should in writing notify any subcontractors, vendors, or other suppliers of company policy regarding employment of the handicapped, and should include the handicap affirmative action clause required by the regulations in any "covered" subcontract (one of $2,500 or more).

Seventh, the contractor must internally disseminate to its own employees its policy of employing and advancing handicapped individuals. The OFCCP has suggested that dissemination include the following: incorporating the policy in the contractor's policy manual; publicizing the policy and how it should be put into force; scheduling meetings with employees to discuss the policy and to explain individual employee responsibility with respect to it; meeting with union officials to inform them of the policy and to request their cooperation; including nondiscrimination clauses in all union contracts; posting the policy on bulletin boards; and including articles featuring handicapped employees in company publications. Finally, a contractor should appoint at each facility someone to be in charge of the handicapped.

3. The Obligation to Develop a Written AAP

Within 120 days of the commencement of a government contract, every contractor or subcontractor holding a contract of $50,000 or more, and having fifty or more employees, must develop a written affirmative action program (AAP) *for each of its establishments*. According to the regulations, the intent of such a program is to detail the contractor's compliance with its affirmative action obligations. Unlike AAPs in the race/sex area, a handicap AAP need contain no statistical analyses of the contractor's work force, nor is there any obligation to set goals or timetables for employing the handicapped.

The regulations state that a contractor has the option of either integrating the handicap AAP into its other affirmative action programs or maintaining a separate program. *In no case, however, should a contractor's handicap AAP be integrated with its race/sex AAP.* Under the handicap regulations, employees are entitled to see a contractor's affirmative action plan on demand. In fact, the contractor must establish and actually post the times and places of permitted inspection. Employers' affirmative action plans in the race/sex area are, of course, highly confidential; and, because their statistical break-downs of the contractor's work force could prove harmful to the company's business interests if disclosed to the wrong people, they should not be shown voluntarily to employees. A contractor should, on the other hand, combine its handicap AAP with its Vietnam Era Veterans Readjustment Assistance Act AAP, since the regulations governing them are for all intents and purposes identical.[7]

A contractor is required to invite all applicants and employees who believe themselves covered by the Rehabilitation Act and who wish to take advantage of the contractor's affirmative action program to identify themselves to the contractor. The contractor must assure the invitees that the submission of information on their physical or medical conditions to the contractor is voluntary, and that the information will be kept confidential and used only for the purpose of discharging the contractor's obligations to employ and advance in employment qualified handicapped persons. This assurance, of crucial importance to the OFCCP, can best be provided by the contractor's posting of a notice. The OFCCP recognizes, however, that the contractor is not obliged to search the medical files of employees or applicants to determine whether it employs any handicapped individuals.

4. The Obligation to Keep Records

A contractor must maintain records for one year detailing any complaints that handicapped persons register concerning their treatment, and describing any actions taken in response to those complaints. Moreover, a contractor must furnish any information that the OFCCP demands in the form in which they demand it. Finally, a contractor must grant OFCCP officials access to its affirmative action records whenever they conduct a compliance review or complaint investigation.

5. The Obligation to Avoid Intimidation

The regulations require a contractor to insure that no person intimidates, threatens, coerces, or discriminates against any person because that person intends to file a complaint under the Act, furnish information to a government official, or assist in any investigation. A contractor must post a notice in each facility to that effect.

The Right to Require Physical Exams and Medical History Inquiries

Perhaps the greatest potential impact of the handicap discrimination laws on personnel practices is in the area of preemployment physicals and medical history inquiries. For years many employers have administered preemployment (or post-employment) physicals and have required applicants to complete detailed medical history questionnaires. The OFCCP regulations do not prohibit requiring an applicant or employee to undergo a preemployment medical examination (provided that it is at the contractor's expense), nor do they prohibit a contractor's use of a detailed, preemployment medical history questionnaire. However, the Rehabilitation Act does affect how such information can be used.

The essence of handicap discrimination law is that employers may not make employment decisions based on generalizations about the class of handicapped persons. Employers must consider only whether an applicant with a given physical or mental condition is capable of performing the *specific* duties of the *specific* job for which he or she applies. Thus, an employer can use preemployment physicals and medical history inquiries only to determine whether applicants are physically and/or mentally capable of performing the duties of the jobs applied for. This requirement presents particular problems with respect to drafting a medical history questionnaire. By its very nature, such a form must ask very general, non-job-related questions. Accordingly, the contractor should make sure that every question in its medical history questionnaire is relevant to at least *one* of the contractor's jobs.

The contractor should include a disclaimer in its medical history questionnaire advising applicants that it will use the information only for purposes permitted by the Rehabilitation Act. The following is an example of such a disclaimer:

Below are a series of questions about your physical condition and health. The purpose of these questions is to help us determine whether you are able to perform the duties of the job you are applying for in such a way that you do not endanger your own safety or the health or safety of other employees. No physical condition is an automatic bar to employment. All circumstances will be considered. Please be assured that your answers will be kept confidential. The only persons who will see your answers are company employees and government officials who have a legitimate need for them.

The Penalties for Noncompliance

What can happen if a contractor violates the Rehabilitation Act and the OFCCP regulations? There are two aspects to that question:

1. What Happens When an Individual Charge of Handicap Discrimination is Filed against a Contractor?

Under the Rehabilitation Act, any handicapped person who believes that a government contractor has failed or refused to comply with its affirmative action obligations or its obligation not to discriminate may file a complaint with the Department of Labor (DOL) within 180 days of the alleged violation. After giving the contractor a chance to resolve the complaint internally (if it has an internal review procedure), the Department of Labor will investigate the complaint. If the investigator finds a violation, the DOL must first attempt to remedy it by a process of conciliation and persuasion. Resolution through this informal procedure is not completed until the contractor has made a commitment in writing to take corrective action. In a refusal-to-hire or a discharge case, the DOL may well require the payment of back pay to the applicant or employee as a part of the remedy.

If the complaint is not resolved through informal means, the DOL has the choice of going to court and suing the contractor for breach of its agreement not to discriminate against the handicapped, or of holding an administrative hearing to determine whether the contractor breached its obligations. If it chooses the latter course, the OFCCP may withhold progress payments on current contracts, cancel or terminate contracts, and, ultimately, debar the contractor from receiving future government contracts.[8] For a few years, the OFCCP favored bringing judicial suits. Now, however, it is taking the administrative hearing/debarment route.

Most courts thus have held that handicapped individuals do not have the right to bring their own private judicial actions against employers under the Rehabilitation Act of 1973. The Supreme Court's recent decision in *Cannon v. University of Chicago*,[9] in which it found a private right of action implicit in the terms of Title IX of the Educational Amendments of 1972, may presage a reversal in policy.[10]

2. What Happens When a Contractor's AAP Does Not Comply with the OFCCP Regulations?

For a long time, the OFCCP did not actively conduct compliance reviews of government contractors' affirmative action programs for the handicapped. Compliance agency officials conducting reviews of race/sex AAPs simply checked to see whether the contractor had any handicap AAP. As long as the contractor could show the compliance officer a document whose title page read "AAP for the Handicapped," the contractor had satisfied its obligations. A contractor's handicap AAP was scrutinized carefully for compliance with the OFCCP regulations only when an OFCCP official reviewed it in connection with the investigation of an individual complaint of handicap discrimination.

Recently, however, the emphasis has shifted from individual complaint resolution to systematic enforcement of the handicap laws. This change has accompanied the recent shift of contract compliance review out of the compliance agencies and into the OFCCP.

In preparation for this shift, the OFCCP in 1978 developed a draft review procedure that compliance officers could use in conducting compliance reviews of handicap AAP's. The OFCCP then scheduled test audits of various contractors, including several in California, to see whether its proposed procedures were valid—and whether contractors were in compliance. The test audits revealed that 90 percent were not.

Under the regulations, if a compliance review demonstrates that a contractor is not in compliance, the OFCCP and contractor must engage in "conciliation and persuasion," which involves negotiations by both sides to decide what action the contractor will take—and when—to bring itself into compliance. If the contractor does not agree in writing to take specific corrective action, the OFCCP will issue an "order to show cause," followed by an administrative complaint, which will lead to an administrative hearing. If a violation is found based on the hearing, the contractor can be debarred from future government contracts.

Avoiding Violations of the Act

1. Avoiding Successful Charges of Individual Discrimination

Employment decisions should be based on an assessment of individual ability to perform the job. *A contractor should not make class decisions.* For example, a contractor should not reject all people with bad backs or heart conditions, regardless of the position applied for. Each individual must be considered on the basis of his or her own abilities in relation to the specific position applied for.

If a contractor uses preemployment physical examinations, it should not allow the examining doctors to make the hiring decisions. Doctors should be asked only for their conclusions about an applicant's physical ability to perform the job applied for. The actual employment decision should be made by the contractor.

Job requirements must be job-related. Physical and mental qualifications required of applicants for given positions must be essential to the proper performance of those positions.

2. Drafting a Successful AAP

According to the draft compliance review procedures mentioned above, compliance reviewers will focus on five areas to determine whether a contractor is minimally in compliance with the Act and the OFCCP regulations. In drafting its AAP, a contractor should address itself to these five areas:

(1) The contractor should make sure that all required notices are posted, *especially* the notice inviting applicants and employees to identify themselves to you as handicapped. Such notices should be posted in areas used both by employees and applicants.

(2) The contractor should develop a specific schedule for reviewing its physical and mental job qualification requirements, put that schedule in its AAP, *and adhere to it.*

(3) The contractor should be sure that the required affirmative action clauses are included in its subcontracts.

(4) The contractor should develop a procedure to review its personnel processes to make sure it is taking the required affirmative action.

(5) The contractor should make contact with recruitment sources for handicapped and list in its AAP the ones contacted.

Conclusion

These, then, are the federal laws concerning the handicapped. They are comprehensive, and they impose significant responsibilities on personnel managers in particular. Violation of the laws can lead to serious consequences for the government contractor. Enforcement will only become tougher in the months and years to follow.

NOTES

1. At present, a bill is pending in Congress that would extend Title VII of the Civil Rights Act to include the handicapped as a protected class. If that bill ultimately passes, all employers, not just federal contractors, will be affected.

2. Any government contractors with contracts in excess of $2,500 are covered by section 503 of the Rehabilitation Act of 1973, 29 U.S.C. § 793 (1975). Recipients of federal financial assistance are covered by section 504 of that Act, 29 U.S.C. § 794 (1975). Because most private employers, except those with CETA programs or other financial aid from the government, are covered by section 503, I will stress that section in the remainder of this article.

3. The OFCCP regulations concerning the Rehabilitation Act are contained at 41 CFR § 60-741.1 *et seq.*

4. In the case of *Trans World Airlines vs. Hardison*, 432 U.S. 63 (1977), the United States Supreme Court took a very narrow view of the extent of the obligations imposed on employers by Title VII to "reasonably accommodate" the religious beliefs of their employees. In that case, the Court held that an employer need not make any accommodation that would cost more than a "de minimis" amount. It remains to be seen whether that restrictive view will be applied to the Rehabilitation Act. The Supreme Court's recent decision in *Southeastern Community College v. Davis*, ——— U.S. ———; 47 U.S.L.W. 4689 (June 11, 1979), suggests that it is still disinclined to impose on employers reasonable accommodation obligations requiring their expenditure of considerable funds. In that case, the Supreme Court held that under section 504 of the Rehabilitation Act, the Department of Health, Education and Welfare, which administers that section, cannot impose an obligation on educational institutions to engage in "reasonable accommodation" to the physical/mental handicaps of beneficiaries of programs or activities that receive federal financial assistance.

5. The case is reported at 77-OFCCP-7-R.

6. The OFCCP has still not ruled on the issue of whether an employer who is forced to hire an applicant who predictably will aggravate a preexisting physical condition may exclude the individual from medical insurance coverage, or provide insurance that *costs* the same as that given to other employees but affords less coverage.

7. The Vietnam Era Veterans Readjustment Assistance Act of 1974, 38 U.S.C. § 2012, requires contractors with contracts of $10,000 or more to take affirmative action to employ and advance in employment veterans of the Vietnam Era and qualified disabled veterans. The OFCCP, which also administers this Act, has issued regulations interpreting it. These regulations begin at 41 CFR § 60-250.1.

8. The OFCCP used to take the position that once it had issued an "order

to show cause" (why a complaint should not issue), it could *automatically* pass over a government contractor for two contracts, without telling the contractor or holding a hearing on whether the contractor had in fact committed a violation. A number of courts have held that such "passovers" are illegal, and the OFCCP has quietly stopped doing it.

9. ——— U.S. ———, 99 S.Ct. 1946 (1979).

10. In *Hart v. County of Alameda*, ——— F.Supp. ———, C-79-0091-WHO (N.D. Cal. Sept. 6, 1979), a federal court, relying on *Cannon*, found a private right of action implicit in section 503 of the Rehabilitation Act. This decision is particularly troublesome for government contractors, because Congress just amended the Rehabilitation Act to provide for the payment of attorneys' fees to successful litigants.

The *Weber* Decision: Summary and Analysis

John J. Gallagher

On June 27, 1979, the Supreme Court issued its decision in *United Steelworkers of America v. Weber*. The Court, by a 5-2 vote, upheld the legality of numerical quotas based on race in voluntary affirmative action programs of private employers.

This article presents a summary of the Court's decision in *Weber* and an analysis of its likely impact on the law of employment discrimination. *Weber* answers many legal questions and provides some protection for employers against reverse discrimination lawsuits. Other questions remain unanswered, however, and the scope of the protection afforded against reverse discrimination claims is by no means clear.

Summary

Background

In 1974, the United Steelworkers of America (USW) and Kaiser Aluminum & Chemical Corporation entered a new collective-bargaining agreement covering fifteen Kaiser plants. The agreement approved an affirmative action program that established on-the-job training programs to teach unskilled production workers the skills

John J. Gallagher is with the law firm of Akin, Gump, Hauer & Feld in Washington, D.C.

necessary to become craft workers. The program was "voluntarily" established by Kaiser and USW, although it was adopted after critical reviews from the Office of Federal Contract Compliance, which monitors affirmative action compliance for federal contractors. The program was modeled on a nationwide consent decree then being created for the steel industry. Selection for the training programs was based on seniority, with 50 percent of the openings reserved for blacks. This racial preference was to exist until the percentage of black craft workers roughly equalled the percentage of blacks in the area's work force.

At Kaiser's plant in Gramercy, Louisiana, thirteen trainees were selected under the affirmative action program—seven black and six white. Prior to 1974, only 1.83 percent of the skilled craft workers at the Gramercy plant were black, even though the work force in the Gramercy area was approximately 39 percent black. The most junior black selected for the program had less seniority than several white workers whose applications for the training program were rejected. Brian F. Weber, one of the rejected white applicants, brought a class action on behalf of the rejected white applicants, alleging that Kaiser's selection process denied access to on-the-job training programs on the basis of race and thus violated sections 703(a) and (d) of Title VII of the Civil Rights Act of 1964, which make it illegal to "discriminate . . . because of . . . race" in hiring and training programs.

Section 703(a), 42 U.S.C. § 2000e-2(a), provides:

> (a) It shall be an unlawful employment practice for an employer—
> (1) to fail or refuse to hire . . . any individual, or otherwise to discriminate against any individual with respect to his compensation, terms, conditions, or privileges of employment, because of such individual's race . . .; or
>
> (2) to limit or classify his employees or applicants for employment in any way which would deprive or tend to deprive any individual of employment opportunities or otherwise adversely affect his status as an employee, because of such individual's race. . . .

Section 703(d), 42 U.S.C. § 2000e-2(d), provides:

> It shall be an unlawful employment practice for any employer [or] labor organization . . . controlling apprenticeship or other training or retraining, including on-the-job training programs to discriminate against any individual because of his race . . . in admission to, or employment in, any program established to provide apprenticeship or other training.

36

Majority Opinion

Justice Brennan wrote the thirteen-page majority opinion in which Justices Stewart, White, Marshall, and Blackmun joined.[1] The opinion emphasized at the outset the narrowness of the Court's holding, limiting the issue decided to "the narrow statutory issue of whether Title VII *forbids* private employers and unions from voluntarily agreeing upon bona fide affirmative action plans that accord racial preferences in the manner and for the purposes provided in the Kaiser-USWA plan." The difficulty facing the Court was the literal language of Title VII, which makes it unlawful to "discriminate . . . because of . . . race" in hiring and in the selection of workers for training programs, and the conflicting statements concerning affirmative action in the legislative history.

In his majority opinion, Justice Brennan acknowledged that Weber's position, premised on the express language of the statute and much legislative history, was "not without force." The majority concluded, however, that Title VII must be read against the background of its legislative history and purpose. Analysis of that legislative history convinced the majority that Congress's goal was to open employment opportunities for minorities, especially blacks; thus it would be inconsistent with the legislative purpose to interpret Title VII to prohibit private affirmative action programs designed to further that goal.

The majority relied in part upon negative implication from another subsection of section 703 to support its conclusion. Section 703(j) provides that nothing in Title VII "shall be interpreted to *require* any employer . . . to grant preferential treatment . . . to any group because of . . . race." Justice Brennan explained that the use of the word "require" rather than "permit" creates "[t]he natural inference . . . that Congress chose not to forbid all voluntary race-conscious affirmative action."

The majority took judicial notice (i.e., accepted as fact without evidence) that construction craft positions had been traditionally race-segregated in our society. This "fact," combined with the extremely low percentage of blacks in craft positions at Kaiser, was found to constitute sufficient justification for the voluntary adoption of the affirmative action plan. The majority did not require that Kaiser admit past discrimination—not even "arguable" past discrimination, as Justice Blackmun would have required in his concurring opinion. Thus, past "societal" discrimination (traditionally segregated job categories), combined with low black representation, sufficed to justify an affirmative action plan without specific evidence, or admission, of discrimination by the employer.

The majority expressly refrained from unqualified endorsement of any actions taken pursuant to an affirmative action plan. The Court noted that the Kaiser-USW plan was a temporary plan designed to eliminate a manifest racial imbalance rather than to maintain a racial balance. The plan did not "unnecessarily trammel" the interests of white workers, e.g., by requiring their discharge or erecting an absolute bar to their advancement. These qualifications to the Court's holding indicate that future cases will evaluate the legality of each affirmative action plan separately in light of such factors as its impact on white workers and its duration.

Concurring Opinion

Justice Blackmun expressed some reservations about Justice Brennan's interpretation of the legislative history but joined in the majority's opinion and judgment because of the practical difficulties he perceived with a literal reading of Title VII. Blackmun noted that an employer and union would be on a "high tightrope without a net beneath them" if they were unable to take voluntary corrective action when faced with facts or statistics suggesting vulnerability to charges of race discrimination under Title VII. Thus Title VII had to be read to permit self-analysis and corrective action, which would necessarily be "race-conscious." Blackmun issued a concurring opinion because he felt that the majority used an overly broad standard to define the circumstances in which an affirmative action program was permissible under Title VII. He referred to the majority's approach as a broad-sweeping "traditionally segregated job category" standard. Blackmun would have preferred a more limited approach requiring an "arguable violation" of Title VII against minorities as a prerequisite to affirmative action in favor of minorities. He acknowledged, however, that the definition of an "arguable" violation could lead to an unproductive semantic debate. He therefore joined in the majority decision.

Dissents

Justices Burger and Rehnquist each wrote a separate dissenting opinion. They both stated that the legislative history did not support the majority's interpretation of Title VII and that Title VII must be read literally to prohibit all race-conscious employment decisions.

Justice Rehnquist was vehement in his dissent, analyzing the legislative history at length and suggesting that the majority's interpretation of the statute was judicial fabrication more appropriate in George Orwell's *1984* than in 1979.

Analysis

The *Weber* decision substantially resolves the issues of "reverse discrimination" in employment under Title VII of the Civil Rights Act of 1964. The decision, however, is basically inconsistent with the result reached one year earlier in the much publicized *Bakke* case,[2] which dealt with reverse discrimination in admission to a federally funded medical school subject to Title VI of the 1964 Civil Rights Act. The *Weber* decision is also very narrow, as the Court expressly emphasized. The decison deals only with the prohibitions on the voluntary conduct of private employers that Congress wrote into Title VII; it does not purport to deal with constitutional issues, such as the extent to which the government can mandate or participate in similar affirmative action programs. The narrowness of the decision on statutory grounds probably enabled the Supreme Court to secure five votes for the majority position, for as Justice Blackmun noted, Congress can amend the statute to change the result if it so chooses.

A majority of the Court in the *Bakke* case had held that racially based numerical quotas in admission to medical school were prohibited by Title VI of the Civil Rights Act of 1964.[3] Virtually identical language in Title VII of the same statute, passed at the same time, has now been interpreted in *Weber* to allow racially based numerical quotas in employment decisions made as part of an affirmative action program. Justice Stewart was the swing vote who sided with the majority in both cases, yet he made no attempt to explain the apparent inconsistency in his position.

The majority opinion in *Weber* cited *Bakke* only once, in a footnote, explaining that Title VI of the 1964 Civil Rights Act contains no provision comparable to Title VII's § 703(j), barring government-required racial preferences.[4] The footnote went on to note that Title VI involved Congress's power over use of federal funds, while Title VII had a different constitutional basis in the Commerce clause. Thus, the Court noted, Title VI and Title VII "cannot be read *in pari materia*." Having made this distinction, however, the majority opinion did not then use it to justify the different results in *Bakke* and *Weber*.

One evident explanation for the different results in *Bakke* and *Weber* is that the Court in *Weber* was aware of our society's history of employment discrimination and was convinced that numerically based affirmative action plans were essential in an employment context to achieve the goals sought by Congress in Title VII. Thus, the Court read Title VII in a broader context—some would say a "result oriented" context—than they had read Title VI of the same statute.

Unresolved Questions

Voluntary race-conscious employment decisions in certain situations are clearly on a firmer legal basis in light of the *Weber* decision. The narrowness of the Court's holding, however, raises many questions. We address these questions below.

When is affirmative action permissible?

Under the *Weber* rationale, voluntary race-conscious affirmative action efforts are permissible under Title VII to remedy "manifest racial imbalance," to break down "old patterns of racial segregation and hierarchy," Yet, the court failed to indicate how an employer may know if its work force is sufficiently imbalanced in job categories having sufficient traditional segregation to warrant affirmative action. Clearly, the imbalance in Kaiser's craft work force was sufficiently conspicuous and traditional to satisfy the Court. Affirmative action might be less justifiable where there are much less dramatic disproportions between black and white representation; the Court clearly intimated disfavor with a plan designed solely to maintain racial balance. Thus, employers and unions should continue to be careful and to undertake thorough self-analysis prior to initiation of voluntary affirmative action programs. Where statistical variations are extreme and the obvious result of past societal discrimination, affirmative action is permissible and appropriate. (Note that the traditional segregation or discrimination need *not* have been the act of the employer; "societal" patterns suffice.) Where the statistical variations and their causes are less clear, however, race-conscious employment decisions may still cause legal difficulties.

What types of affirmative action are permissible?

The Court emphasized the fact that the Kaiser-USW plan did not "unnecessarily trammel" the interests of white employees, indicating that a plan which did have a dramatic or preemptive impact on white employees could be viewed in a different light. There is no apparent basis in the statutory language for this limitation on the Court's holding; apparently, it is simply an element in defining whether the "good discrimination" permitted by the statute is "good enough." Nonetheless, numerical quotas on entry into a training program are permissible.

Although the Court did not expressly emphasize the role of the USW in the Kaiser affirmative action plan, the fact that Weber's union was intimately involved in the design of the plan may well have been a factor in the Court's evaluation of its impact on white employees. Where a union represents incumbent employees, it should certainly be brought into any discussions concerning the creation of an affirmative action plan. While a union may at times raise obstacles or objections to an employer's proposed affirmative action plan, the union does represent important employee interests and may share in any Title VII liability arising out of collectively bargained employment practices.

The temporary nature of the Kaiser-USW affirmative action plan was an important, and possibly indispensable, element. A permissible affirmative action plan should, therefore, be addressed to eliminating the effects of past societal discrimination and should cease when that result is achieved. Permanent plans designed solely to maintain racial balance do not seem to meet the Court's criteria.

It is more difficult to assess the various approaches to affirmative action that may be permissible. The key element in the Court's view is apparently to minimize the impact on innocent white employees. While a 50 percent quota for blacks is permissible, it is questionable whether an exclusionary 100 percent quota would be acceptable unless it were sharply defined and limited to minimize its impact on innocent whites. The training context in which *Weber* arose was a relatively easy one for the Court; it noted that Brian Weber was not discharged, nor was he forever barred from entry into other training programs. More difficult situations will be presented in hiring and promotion cases where the impact on the whites not chosen may be more dramatic. The Supreme Court has provided no effective guidance on how such cases should be decided. It is clear, however, that Title VII permits affirmative action; the burden in future cases will be on the white employee plaintiff to show that a particular affirmative action program has crossed the ill-defined line into impermissible action.

In effect, future cases will turn on the total factual context in which they arise: the extent of past discrimination, the degree of imbalance in the work force, the nature of the proposed affirmative action, and its impact on affected whites. This has the unfortunate consequence of ensuring further litigation, since each potential plaintiff is likely to regard his or her case as stronger than the last. It also denies to employers advance guidance on how to structure their affirmative action programs to avoid legal difficulties.

What is the status of government-mandated affirmative action programs?

Section 730(j) of Title VII states that Title VII shall not be interpreted "to require any employer . . . to grant preferential treatment . . . because of . . . race . . . on account of an imbalance" by race between the employer's work force and the available community work force. The discussion of this provison in the majority opinion may raise questions about the continued viability of government-mandated affirmative action programs. The majority stated that:

> [This] section was designed to prevent . . . Title VII from being interpreted in such a way as to lead to undue "Federal Government interference with private businesses because of some Federal employee's ideas about racial balance or imbalance."[5]

The court went on to emphasize Congress's desire to avoid "undue federal regulation of private businesses" and to avoid a statute that "would augment the powers of the Federal Government and diminish traditional management prerogatives. . . ."

These comments may indicate the Court's view that Congress has disapproved of any government-mandated affirmative action programs. The comments strike forcefully against any argument that Congress has somehow implicitly approved of the federal government's mandatory affirmative action programs for federal contractors. The Court's decision thus raises questions about the legality of such programs.

The arguments in response to these questions are readily available. First of all, the federally required affirmative action programs are mandated by an Executive Order of the President, E.O. 11246, as amended. The restriction of section 703(j) of Title VII says simply that nothing contained "in Title VII" shall be interpreted to require racial preferences. Since the Executive Order is not "in Title VII," the argument goes, section 703(j) has no application. This argument is not without force if Title VII and the Executive Order are legally independent. The Fifth Circuit decision in *Weber*, however, expressly stated that the Executive Order "may not override contradictory congressional expressions" in Title VII.[6] The Supreme Court did not find it necessary to reach this issue in its *Weber* decision. Thus, the issue remains open for future cases.

There also exists a constitutional argument independent of the statutory basis for challenging government-mandated affirmative action programs. Since the *Weber* case did not involve any formal or official government action, the Court was careful to avoid implying any views on whether the Due Process or Equal Protection clauses of the Constitution might prohibit government actions or requirements based on racial classifications. The views of five members of the Court on these constitutional issues were revealed in *Bakke*; the four minority Justices in that case (Marshall, Brennan, Blackmun, and White) would allow race-conscious government action, including numerical quotas, to remedy past societal discrimination. Justice Powell would allow the government to consider race as one factor among many in certain decisions but would prohibit numerical goals or quotas. The views of the remaining Justices (Burger, Rehnquist, Stewart, and Stevens) on the constitutional issues are unknown. As long as the composition of the Court remains the same, there is an apparent majority (Powell, Marshall, Brennan, Blackmun, and White) that would allow the government to adopt the concept of affirmative action, i.e., race-conscious decision making, to remedy past discrimination, but there is no majority (because of Powell's disapproval of numerical goals or quotas) on the form such affirmative action might take. Since the current government-mandated affirmative action programs rely heavily on numerical goals and statistical "imbalance," their constitutionality remains an unresolved question after *Bakke* and *Weber*.

What is the status of affirmative action programs in government employment?

Government employment at the federal, state, and local levels now constitutes a major element of this nation's work force. Government employment decisions at all levels are subject to the constitutional requirements of due process and equal protection discussed above that do not apply to the decisions of private employers. The constitutional issues surrounding what the government can require of private employers, therefore, also surround the question of what government itself can do in its own employment decisions. Thus, *Weber* cannot be read to constitute blanket approval of affirmative action plans in government employment.

What is the status of previous consent decrees or judgments requiring affirmative action?

Even if the *Weber* decision had disapproved of voluntary affirmative action plans, it would have had little impact on affirmative action measures imposed pursuant to previous Consent Decrees or Judgments. This is because such affirmative action is in response to a judicial finding of actual past discrimination that must be remedied, or in the case of Consent Decrees, a judicial determination that the remedies agreed to by the parties are appropriate in light of all the evidence in the court record. This judicial involvement places such affirmative action on a much stronger legal basis than simple voluntary affirmative action.

The status of conciliation agreements with government agencies such as the Equal Employment Opportunity Commission (EEOC) is somewhat different, since such agreements do not have a judicial stamp of approval. However, they usually do involve at least some form of government "finding" that past discrimination has occurred and that remedial action is necessary. Thus, they are not simply directed at remedying "societal" discrimination, but the allegedly illegal actions of a particular employer. They are distinct, therefore, from more generalized government-mandated affirmative action programs designed to promote a general racial balance in the work force.

What is the effect of the Civil Rights Act of 1866, 42 U.S.C. § 1981?

Employment discrimination cases are usually filed under two separate statutes, Title VII of the Civil Rights Act of 1964 and the Civil Rights Act of 1866, 42 U.S.C. § 1981 (hereinafter referred to as § 1981). The Supreme Court has previously held that § 1981 protects white employees from employment discrimination based on race.[7] The Supreme Court has also held that these two statutes constitute independent legal remedies for employment discrimination, with independent legal implications.[8] While a plaintiff can recover damages only once for the same injury, most employment discrimination cases are filed under both statutes in an effort to ensure that the plaintiff has every avenue of attack open to him or her. For reasons not disclosed in the record, Brian Weber filed his lawsuit only under Title VII and did not invoke § 1981. His case was decided, therefore, only under Title VII. Since § 1981 is in theory independent of Title VII, and has an independent legislative history, the question arises whether § 1981 might still prohibit the Kaiser-USW affirmative action plan. The Supreme Court did not touch upon this question in *Weber*. While several lower courts held that § 1981 should be interpreted "to avoid undesirable substantive law conflicts"[9] with Title VII, the Supreme Court has not yet addressed the possibility for such conflicts. Thus the effect of § 1981 remains unknown.

Conclusion

The *Weber* decision represents a significant victory for proponents of affirmative action programs. That victory, however, is a narrow one and leaves many issues for resolution in future cases.

NOTES

1. Justices Powell and Stevens did not participate in the decision. Justice Powell was absent for surgery when the case was argued; Justice Stevens's former law firm reportedly represents Kaiser.

2. *Regents of the University of California v. Bakke*, 438 U.S. 265 (1978).

3. Justices Burger, Rehnquist, Stewart, Stevens, and Powell formed this majority in *Bakke*. Justice Powell went further than his colleagues in *Bakke* and decided that racially based numerical quotas in government programs were prohibited by the Equal Protection Clause of the Constitution as well as the prohibitions of Title VI, which he found to be coextensive.

4. Slip Opinion at 10-11, n. 6.

5. Slip Opinion at 10, quoting 110 Cong. Rec. at 14314 (remarks of Sen. Miller) (footnote omitted).

6. 563 F.2d 216, 227 (5th Cir. 1977).

7. *McDonald v. Santa Fe Transportation Co.* 427 U.S. 273 (1976).

8. *Johnson v. Railway Express Agency, Inc.*, 421 U.S. 454 (1974); *Alexander v. Gardner-Denver Co.*, 415 U.S. 36 (1974). The procedural prerequisites to filing are more complex under Title VII, while the plaintiff's burden

of proof may be heavier under § 1981, since several courts have held that intentional discrimination must be shown to establish a violation of § 1981.

9. *Walters v. Wisconsin Steel Works*, 502 F.2d 1309, 1316 (7th Cir. 1974) *cert. denied* 425 U.S. 997 (1976).

Age Discrimination in Employment Act Amendments of 1978: An Overview

Duane C. Aldrich and Edmund M. Kneisel

(This article was written in 1978. References to time should be interpreted with this in mind.)

On April 6, 1978, President Carter signed into law the Age Discrimination in Employment Act Amendments of 1978. Slightly less than one month later, Congress, by its silence, approved the President's Reorganization Plan No. 1 of 1978, transferring age discrimination enforcement and regulatory functions from the Department of Labor to the Equal Employment Opportunity Commission. Thus, in the space of one month, the legislative branch of government has approved the two most significant substantive and procedural changes in employment practices affecting older workers since the passage of the Age Discrimination in Employment Act of 1967 (ADEA), 29 U.S.C. §§ 621, *et seq.*

Duane C. Aldrich graduated from Harvard Law School in 1968 and is a partner in the law firm of Kilpatrick, Cody, Rogers, McClatchey & Regenstein in Atlanta.

Edmund M. Kneisel is a 1974 graduate of the University of Georgia Law School and is associated with the Atlanta firm of Kilpatrick, Cody, Rogers, McClatchey & Regenstein.

The approach of Congress to passage of the amendments was aptly described by Congressman Erlenborn in the *Congressional Record:* "[W]hen you see a steamroller coming down the street, the only smart thing to do is get out of the way." This was echoed by Senator Percy, who stated, "I have never voted on a bill which I have more reservations and questions about than this bill." Nevertheless, Senator Percy and 62 of the 72 senators casting votes did so in favor of the bill. It remains to be seen whether these amendments will achieve the desired goal of allowing productive older workers to continue to contribute their talents and experience to the workforce; or whether, as feared by Senator Stevenson, the amendments will create a private sector "civil service" system which will erode economic efficiency and contribute to unemployment:

> I sense we in Congress are moving toward placing the whole Nation under a kind of quasi-civil service set of rules that will only further erode the efficiency of our economic system . . . .
>
> Legislation is not always the answer to everything we disapprove of, and, in this case, I feel employers and employees are better able to make retirement decisions than is the Federal Government . . . .
>
> We should do far more to take advantage of the skills and experience of the elderly—but not at the expense of the economic system as a whole and those who are young. I am not so worried about big business; it usually copes, usually by charging us all a little more for its wares. I am concerned, however, about those unemployed, who to borrow from David Broder, are "not all right, Jack."

This article will briefly trace the portions of the amendments which affect private sector employment. Important procedural amendments to the ADEA will be discussed in the last section of this article. The major substantive amendments will be discussed in subheadings on mandatory retirement and pension benefits. Detailed recommendations concerning needed changes to insurance, pension and other welfare benefit plans are beyond the scope of this article; however, whenever possible, we will note specific problem areas.

Mandatory Retirement Before Age 70 Unlawful

The first amendment to the ADEA has received little publicity, but it is extremely noteworthy as an expression of legislative intent designed to overrule the recent Supreme Court opinion in *United Air Lines, Inc. v. McMann.*[1] In *McMann*, the court upheld the validity of a "bona fide" early retirement provision in a company benefit plan. The amendment provides clearly that no seniority system or benefit plan "shall require or permit the involuntary retirement of any individual [within the protected group] . . . because of the age of such individual." Section 2(a) of Amendments, amending 29 U.S.C. § 623(f)(2).

Under this amendment, mandatory provisions in employee benefit plans requiring termination of active employment before age 65 were invalidated as of the enactment date of the amendments. Section 2(b) of this amendment contains an exception deferring the effective date of section 2(a) where mandatory retirement provisions are established by collective bargaining agreements in effect on September 1, 1977. On June 6, 1978, the Department of Labor issued an opinion letter limiting applicability of this exception to age 65-70 retirement provisions only. The Department has stated that "the delay in effective date for certain collective bargaining agreements does not apply to involuntary retirement below age 65." This collective bargaining exception does protect mandatory age 65 retirement provisions which would otherwise be invalidated by the next amendment discussed.

The most significant amendment to the ADEA, like the foregoing amendment, will have a substantial impact on retirement plans and pension plan managers. This highly publicized amendment expands the "protected group" from ages 40 to 65 to include all employees between the ages of 40 and 70. Section 3(a) of Amendments, amending 29 U.S.C. § 631. This extension of ADEA coverage changes the "traditional" mandatory retirement age from 65 to 70 effective January 1, 1979. Thus, while early retirement provisions in current plans are invalidated immediately, mandatory age 65 retirement provisions remain valid until next year. Thereafter, with limited exceptions, no benefit plan provision may require an employee to leave active employment before age 70.

As previously noted, one exception to age 70 retirement is the saving provision protecting retirement provisions in current collective bargaining agreements. Age 65-70 retirement provisions in such agreements remain valid until the date of expiration of the agreement or January 1, 1980, whichever occurs first. Of course, this provision applies only to plans in effect as of September 1, 1977. Plans negotiated after that date may not require early retirement and must allow employees to work until age 70 after January 1, 1979.

The amendments also contain a specific exception permitting retirement of employees between the ages of 65 and 70 when three conditions are fulfilled:

1. The prospective retiree must be employed in a bona fide executive or high policy-making job position;
2. The prospective retiree must be employed in that position for at least two years before retirement;
3. The prospective retiree must be entitled on retirement to at least $27,000 in annual pension receipts.

Congressional intent concerning the vague contours of this exemption is clarified somewhat by legislative history. The House-Senate Conference Committee Report reveals that the conferees intend the $27,000 ceiling to be calculated by excluding amounts attributable to Social Security, employee contributions, and pension receipts from previous employers. Similarly, the conferees clearly state that the exemption is designed only to apply to top-level management personnel such as the head of a "significant and substantial local or regional operation"; or the "heads of major departments or divisions" and their "immediate subordinates" who may exercise "executive authority"; or personnel not in "line" management positions who nevertheless "play a significant role" in policy-making decisions. Obviously, the application of these vague standards must be determined on a case-by-case basis. Moreover, in light of the detailed statement of legislative intent it is likely that the courts will carefully examine any efforts to force top-level managers to retire before age 70.

The amendments invalidating mandatory early retirement and age 65 retirement practices are the two major substantive amendments affecting the private sector. The prohibitions of the ADEA and the previous exceptions contained in the Act remain unchanged. Unless the collective bargaining exception applies, companies must amend plans requiring employees to retire at age 65 by January 1, 1979. Retirement plans requiring mandatory retirement before age 65 must be amended immediately. As will be discussed in the next section of this article, the extent to which retirement plans must be adjusted to allow employees to accrue benefits after age 65 is uncertain.

The Amendments' Impact on Retirement and Benefit Plans

As noted, the age-70 provisions of the amendments will not take effect until January 1, 1979. Legislative history indicates that this delay is designed to provide enough lead time to allow companies to bring their policies and benefit plans into compliance with the law. In fact, Senator Percy indicated that deferring the effective date "was one reason why many of us felt that we could vote for the bill, even with serious reservations, because we do have a full year before its effective date to study the matter further." It is very likely that the primary area of "study" will be how to adjust retirement and welfare benefit plans to account for the increased costs of continued employment of older workers after January 1, 1979.

The amendments themselves do not mention this potentially complex issue, but they leave intact the exception in the 1967 Act permitting employers "to observe the terms of a . . . bona fide employee benefit plan such as a retirement, pension, or insurance plan, which is not a subterfuge to evade the purposes" of the Act. 29 U.S.C. § 623(f)(2). Unfortunately, there are no reported cases considering the extent to which this exception permits employers to reduce insurance and welfare benefits coverage for older employees. The only cases considering this exception dealt with the mandatory early retirement issue. As mentioned before, those cases, such as *United Air Lines, Inc. v. McMann*, permitting involuntary termination of employment pursuant to early retirement provisions of benefit plans have been effectively overruled by the amendments.

In *McMann*, the court decided that a plan which contained a mandatory early retirement provision in effect before enactment of the 1967 Act could not be considered a subterfuge to avoid the purposes of that Act. Since this specific result in *McMann* has been overruled, it is likely that the *McMann* reasoning could not be relied upon to protect plans which now provide for reduction or elimination of health care and insurance benefits after age 65. The legislative history supports Congressman Waxman's conclusion that any reduction in such benefits, if extreme and if not based on sound actuarial principles, would be considered illegal:

> In the absence of actuarial data which clearly demonstrates that the costs of [benefits] . . . are uniquely burdensome to the employer, such a policy constitutes discrimination and a conscious effort to evade the purposes of the act.

> While the Conference Committee did not specifically address the status of health benefits to older workers protected under this act, it is the intent of this Congress to prevent both open and subtle forms of age discrimination. Exceptions should only be applied in the strictest sense and only with full justification and cause.

Senator Javits offered the only practical guidance in this area by stating that reduction of benefits for older workers would be considered legal "where the actual amount of payment made, or cost incurred [by the employer] in behalf of an older worker is equal to that made or incurred in behalf of a younger worker . . . ."

Unfortunately, neither Senator Javits nor any other congressman explained how this comparative-benefits formula should be calculated. For example, some employers may wish to implement an abrupt reduction of benefits at a specific age, whereas others may establish a gradual reduction of benefits for each year worked after a certain age. Assuming an abrupt reduction of benefits at a specific age, such as age 65, is permissible, what comparative cost figures should be used to measure the benefits reduction? There are a number of potentially viable alternatives: average cost for all workers; average cost for workers within the protected group (ages 40-70) vis-à-vis other workers; or average cost for age 64 employees. Perhaps the least obtrusive method of altering benefits would be to gradually reduce benefits for older workers based on the average cost of insuring workers within particular age bands. Any abrupt reduction at a specific age, if not actuarially based, will invite litigation under the ADEA.

Another unsettled question concerns the issue of whether certain types of benefits may be reduced or eliminated altogether while others remain in effect. For instance, some employers may desire to eliminate company-funded life insurance coverage but not group health or disability programs funded partly by employee contributions. Obviously, the approach least likely to invite litigation would be to leave all welfare benefit plans in full force and effect. This would satisfy older workers, but it might in turn generate complaints from younger employees and even employees within the protected group who must bear the added expense of insurance coverage for employees over age 65.

Senator Javits encouraged the Department of Labor to issue "comprehensive regulations" on these and other unsettled issues; however, preliminary inquiry indicates that the Department does not plan to issue any substantive regulations soon. Despite the broad regulatory authority set forth in 29 U.S.C. § 628, the only regulations issued to date relate to record-keeping requirements rather than substantive matters. The Department has issued a series of interpretive bulletins and opinion letters and will likely continue to do so, but the extent to which these interpretations may be approved by the courts is questionable. The transfer of ADEA regulatory and enforcement authority to the EEOC may lead to promulgation of substantive regulations by that agency; however, employers should not anticipate any clear administrative guidance on these issues soon.

In contrast to the uncertainty concerning welfare benefit plans, the legislative history reveals that Congress apparently understood that the age 70 amendments would not affect "pension benefits" accrual after the "normal retirement age" set forth in current retirement plans under the Employee Retirement Income Security Act of 1974 (ERISA). The impact of the amendments on other retirement benefits is uncertain.

In two letters to the House and Senate Committees studying the amendments, Donald Elisburg, Assistant Secretary of Labor, stated quite clearly that "the proposed amendment to the upper age limit . . . would in no manner affect the definition of the term 'normal retirement age' in Section 3(24) of ERISA." In these letters, Elisburg answered several specific inquiries concerning the proposed amendments. His answers may be summarized as follows:

- Employers will not be required to credit years of service after the "normal retirement age" established for purposes of pension benefit accrual under ERISA;
- The amount of periodic benefits paid at actual retirement need not be adjusted to account for continued employment after "normal retirement age";
- Plans presently providing for payment of benefits at a specified age could be amended to provide that no benefits will be paid before "actual retirement" without violating either ERISA or the ADEA;
- Except for plans which allow continued accrual of benefits for employees who work after age 65, the increase in the upper age limit will achieve pension cost savings resulting from added interest and shorter payment periods because of reduced life expectancies of workers after "actual retirement";
- Cutting off benefit accruals after "normal retirement age" will be legal under the "bona fide retirement plan" exception of the act.

During the final Senate debate on the amendments, Senator Williams cited the Elisburg letter as setting forth the Department of Labor's position on these matters. He added that transfer of ADEA enforcement to the EEOC should not change these basic policy guidelines.

In a colloquy between Senators Javits and Williams, both men stated that the ADEA amendments would not require modification of either a defined benefit or defined contribution plan that eliminates continued benefit accruals after "normal retirement age." Senator

Javits addressed the following question concerning this point to Senator Williams:

> I want to ask our distinguished committee chairman whether he agrees that an employer will be permitted to maintain a defined contribution plan . . . which precludes employer and, if applicable, employee contributions . . . subsequent to . . . the plan's normal retirement age.

Senator Williams answered unequivocally, "Yes," adding that "employers will not be required to continue contributions to either defined benefit or defined contribution plans for employees who continue working beyond a plan's normal retirement age." Williams stated that this assessment of the impact of the amendments on retirement plans was based on Elisburg's letter and was consistent with the position of the Department of Labor.

The senators' statements concerning defined contribution plans are clear, but it is not at all certain that Elisburg's letter was addressed to problems involving such plans. If so, then the letter represents a departure from the Department of Labor's previous position distinguishing between defined benefit and defined contribution plans. One year before enactment of the amendments, the Department of Labor issued an opinion letter in which the Administrator of the Wage and Hour Division stated the following:

> [W]here a retirement plan is funded by defined contributions, as in a money purchase or deferred profit-sharing plan, the age of an employee when hired makes no difference in the employer's contributions. In a defined contribution plan, the employer does not have to fund for a specific level of benefits, and the benefit received by an employee at retirement equals only the value of the contributions made on his behalf. Thus neither actuarial considerations nor age affect the level of an employer's contributions. Accordingly, *we would consider the exclusion of a newly hired older worker from a defined contribution plan to be a violation of the ADEA that is not excused under Section 4(f)(2).* [emphasis added]

Similarly, in 1969, the Department of Labor issued a formal interpretation concerning the applicability of the bona fide plan exception to "profit sharing plans." In this interpretation, the Department stated that such plans "would not appear" to be within the section 4(f)(2) exception, noting that the exception "may apply" if the "essential purpose of a plan financed from profits [is] to provide retirement benefits to employees."

There is no mention in the Elisburg letter or in the legislative history of these previous interpretations. As a result, there is no clear statement that the Department intends to abandon the previous distinction between defined benefit and defined contribution plans. On the other hand, there is likewise no mention in the legislative history that the Department had not previously interpreted the bona fide plan exception to permit complete elimination of pension accruals for older workers without some actuarial justification.

The Department also addressed the question of reduction of "pension, retirement, or insurance benefits" for "older workers." The Department stated that "lesser amounts" of benefits could be provided, but indicated that any reduction in benefits might be subject to question if not based on an actuarial formula. The interpretation sets forth the following comparative costs formula for determining the validity of benefits reduction:

> A retirement, pension, or insurance plan will be considered in compliance with the statute where the actual amount of payment made, or cost incurred, in behalf of an older worker is equal to that made or incurred in behalf of a younger worker, even though the older worker may thereby receive a lesser amount of pension or retirement benefits, or insurance coverage.

This comparative cost formula is the same formula cited by Senator Javits in discussing welfare benefits reductions. The Senator did not reference the source of this formula, but he quoted it in full, including the language concerning pension and retirement benefit plans. Nevertheless, from the context of his remarks, it is clear that Javits intended only the comparative benefits calculation to be applied to welfare benefits reductions. Without citing any comparative benefits analysis, Secretary Elisburg stated quite clearly in his letter that additional pension benefit accruals may be legally eliminated after a plan's "normal retirement age" without liability under the ADEA and without any actuarial adjustment. As a result, to the extent the Labor Department may have abandoned the conflicting 1969 interpretation concerning actuarial justification for a defined benefit plan reduction, it may have changed its position with respect to defined contribution plans as well.

The interpretation of the new amendments and the legality of pension plan adjustments made necessary by those amendments is ultimately a matter for the courts. The extent to which the courts will rely on the arguably inconsistent legislative history is questionable. Pension managers should be cautioned that considering the possible tax consequences of pension plan changes without considering the legal consequences of those changes under the ADEA might create serious problems if those changes are later ruled illegal by the courts.

It appears Congress intended that minor adjustments in plans eliminating mandatory retirement before age 70 would not require prior IRS approval. Such a change could be accomplished simply by notifying employees and sending a summary of the change to the Department of Labor. Unfortunately, the legislative history concerning this procedural issue is unclear. The only mention of this point was Congressman Findley's statement that he was told the IRS "would probably inform the public that such amendments would be administratively allowed without submission to the Service." Absent clearer administrative guidance from the IRS, employers should be wary of making any changes in qualified pension plans without consulting tax counsel first. Of course, even if a plan is submitted to the IRS for approval, the qualification of the plan for favorable tax treatment will not guarantee favorable treatment by the Department of Labor, the EEOC, or the courts in suits under the ADEA.

Until the various administrative agencies, including the Department of Labor, the IRS, and the EEOC, make some rulings on these unsettled issues, any recommendation concerning changes in benefit plans would be premature. Even if administrative rulings, regulations, and interpretive bulletins are consistent with the Javits-Elisburg guidelines, employers should be cautioned that following those guidelines will not automatically insulate pension plan changes from attack. Senator Stevenson stated his belief that the amendments are an "invitation to litigation," and it is quite possible that any plan which terminates or reduces welfare or retirement benefits after age 65 will be challenged in court. One hopes that lawsuits attacking benefits plans which are consistent with the Javits-Elisburg guidelines will be unsuccessful.

The Amendments Ease Procedural Requirements for Litigants

The remaining amendments to the ADEA within the scope of this article are procedural only. The first amendment simply confirms the opinion of the Supreme Court that persons seeking monetary relief shall be entitled to a trial by jury.[2] Moreover, based on the comments of the Conference Committee, the amendment goes beyond the *Pons* ruling by allowing trial by jury of "any issue of fact" pertinent to monetary relief. According to the Conference Committee, this amendment permits jury consideration of a plaintiff's entitlement to wages, fringe, and other job-related benefits, and also his entitlement to "liquidated damages" if the jury finds a "willful violation" of the Act.

The availability of jury trials in age discrimination lawsuits applies to individual lawsuits, not Department of Labor "pattern and practice" cases. In addition, the legislative history of this amendment also supports the proposition that punitive damages are not recoverable in actions brought pursuant to the ADEA. As a result, while the jury trial amendment will create uncertainty for the courts and for attorneys unaccustomed to presenting employment discrimination issues to a jury, this amendment should not affect the basic components of a plaintiff's potential monetary recovery.[3]

The next procedural amendment is more technical. It affects a defense presently available in many age discrimination lawsuits: that a plaintiff's claim is "jurisdictionally barred" because of failure to file a timely notice of intent to sue within 180 days after the alleged act of discrimination against him.[4]

The actual impact of the amendment on the 180-day rule may be slight. The amendment preserves the 180-day filing requirement but provides that an individual seeking relief must file a "charge alleging unlawful discrimination" with the Secretary rather than a "notice" of an intent to bring suit. This filing requirement is now more analogous to the requirement for written "charges" with the EEOC under Title VII of the Civil Rights Act of 1964.

The "substance" of the amendment must be derived from the Conference Committee report rather than from language of the amendment itself. In the report, the conferees state that the amendment is not intended to alter the "basic purpose" of the 180-day rule. On the other hand, the report includes the comment that the " 'charge' requirement is not a jurisdictional prerequisite to maintaining an action." The conferees specifically state that this filing requirement is subject to "equitable modification."

Several courts have already ruled that the 180-day notice-filing requirement is subject to equitable modification. To date, these cases have generally been limited to instances where an employee is not properly informed of his ADEA rights,[5] is misled concerning filing requirements,[6] or continues to negotiate with the offending employer concerning another position.[7] Given this trend of authority, the modification of the "notice" filing language may not significantly alter the 180-day defense in most jurisdictions. Nevertheless, approval of the "equitable modification" approach by the conferees indicates that personnel managers should be well aware of the various administrative requirements concerning notice posting, record keeping, and other procedural matters under the ADEA. Noncompliance with such regulations, even if unintentional, might enable an employee to successfully resist a 180-day-rule defense.

Similarly, all managers involved in personnel decisions should be instructed to clearly communicate adverse personnel decisions to employees. Once a decision has been made, any conduct by a company official which might lead an employee to believe the decision could be subject to change or was not "final" might result in an indefinite extension of the 180-day charge-filing period. Of course, the statute of limitations will ultimately bar unfiled claims, but the value of prompt resolution of claims while records are available and memories are fresh should not be underestimated.

The last procedural amendment to the Act relates specifically to the foregoing charge-filing amendment and provides quite simply that the statute of limitations otherwise incorporated in the ADEA is tolled for a maximum period of one year while the Department of Labor attempts conciliation of the "charge." This amendment clarifies previously unsettled law and does not constitute a significant alteration of procedure. By incorporating a specific one-year maximum tolling provision, the amendment may encourage more thorough conciliation efforts.

Of course, the actual effect of the tolling provision will likely not be felt until the EEOC becomes actively involved in enforcement of the Act. The transfer of authority to the EEOC will create administrative delays at first and might ultimately create even more complex problems when the question of ADEA enforcement conflicts with affirmative action on behalf of other protected classes of employees.

The ADEA Amendments of 1978, coupled with EEOC enforcement of the Act, may generate substantial difficulties over the short term for personnel and employee benefits managers. Nevertheless, from the viewpoint of a trial attorney, the amendments finally passed by Congress are not nearly as troublesome as some of the initial proposals. For instance, jury trials are allowed, but the amendment does not permit recovery of compensatory damages for pain and suffering or punitive damages. Similarly, the 180-day and "state deferral" rules have been retained, thereby reaffirming congressional intent to encourage relatively prompt consideration of age discrimination claims. But the elimination of mandatory early retirement and the inclusion of persons between the ages of 65 and 70 within the protected age group will have a very significant effect on corporate personnel policy and pension planning. These amendments emphasize the necessity for developing careful guidelines concerning the treatment and evaluation of senior employees.

NOTES

1. ____ U.S. ____, 98 S. Ct. 444 (1977).

2. See *Lorillard v. Pons*, ____ U.S. ____, 98 S. Ct. 866 (1978).

3. See, e.g., *Dean v. American Security Ins. Co.*, 559 F.2d 1036 (5th Cir. 1977); *Rogers v. Exxon Research & Engineering Co.*, 550 F.2d 834 (3d Cir. 1977).

5. *Charlier v. S.C. Johnson & Son, Inc.*, 556 F.2d 761 (5th Cir. 1977).

6. *Dartt v. Shell Oil Co.*, 539 F.2d 1256 (10th Cir. 1976).

7. *Bonham v. Dresser Industries, Inc.*, 569 F.2d 183 (3d Cir. 1978).

A Tightrope for Employers—
Affirmative Action Post-*Bakke*

Stanley Mazaroff

The tightrope employers have walked between preferential affirmative action for minorities and females as groups and equal opportunity for each individual has been made no less precarious as a result of the *Bakke* decision. *Bakke*, of course, was not an employment case, and the holding of the Court that Bakke was excluded from medical school unlawfully by the University of California's special admissions program cannot easily be superimposed on an employment setting. To blithely read—as apparently some public officials have—*Bakke* as a carte blanche endorsement of the EEOC's and OFCCP's preferential hiring policies for minorities and females is simply unrealistic. On the other hand, nothing in the Court's opinion expressly halted the continued use of either governmental or voluntary affirmative action programs. The federal government policies, at least for the time being, remain intact. Thus, *Bakke* cannot be reduced to a decision clearly for or against affirmative action in employment. And the dilemma over whether an employer must, as a practical matter, select a minimally qualified black over a better qualified white in order to satisfy the government's affirmative action policies remains up in the

Mr. Mazaroff, a partner in the firm of Venable, Baetjer and Howard in Baltimore, Maryland, specializes in equal employment and labor matters. He is a graduate of the University of Maryland Law School.

air. Until the Court provides further guidance on this issue, employers should continue to balance their equal opportunity and affirmative action obligations delicately.

Although *Bakke* was not an employment case, the various opinions of the Justices often were grounded on explications of equal employment law. In the body of their opinions and in lengthy footnotes, the Justices debated the central question of whether civil rights laws must be essentially colorblind or color conscious. They argued over similarly crucial issues, such as whether the right of each applicant to race-free employment consideration supersedes the interest of providing preferential treatment for minority groups; whether legal findings of unlawful discrimination are a necessary predicate for racially preferential hiring systems; and whether employers on their own can adopt affirmative action plans in order to grant preference to victims of societal discrimination. Given the division of opinion regarding the legality of the medical school's admissions program, it should come as no surprise that the Justices were divided over the answers to these fundamental questions as well as to the underlying meaning of many of their own landmark equal employment cases.

Justice Stevens, writing for Chief Justice Burger and Justices Stewart and Rehnquist (in an opinion hereinafter referred to as the Stevens view), perceived the 1964 Civil Rights Act as requiring strict racial neutrality—in other words, colorblindness. The opposite view was expressed by Justice Brennan, writing for Justices White, Marshall, and Blackmun (the Brennan view), who contended that equal opportunity law not only permitted but encouraged voluntary race-conscious action to remedy society wrongs, even at the expense of white applicants. The middle view, which I interpret as being closer to the Stevens view, was espoused by Justice Powell. Absent past unlawful discrimination, he rejected the use of strict racial lines in making selection decisions but accepted the flexible use of race as one factor among many that can be considered in the selection process when cultural diversity represents a compelling interest. The views of Powell, Stevens, and Brennan became frequently entangled and obscure, and one cannot leave the opinion with any certainty as to what lies ahead. Nevertheless, one can begin to faintly discern arising out of the *Bakke* debate certain equal employment principles to which at least a majority of the Justices appear to subscribe and which, therefore, should bear strongly on the future development of the law in this area.

The precepts that very tentatively appear to be supported by at least a majority of the Court are as follows. First, there is no requirement arising solely out of Title VII of the 1964 Civil Rights Act for employers to grant preferential treatment to minority applicants pursuant to affirmative action plans. Second, under Title VII the right of each individual to equality of opportunity without regard to race or sex is supreme over the interest of minority groups to increase their work force representation. Third, preferential hiring ratios set forth in affirmative action plans under Executive Order 11246 are legal insofar as they are predicated on findings of previous discrimination. Fourth, when there is a finding under Title VII that an employer has violated equal employment law, racial or sexual preferences can be used to remedy the past violation; conversely, absent proven violations of equal employment law, an employer cannot give racial preference to one racial or ethnic group over another in order to heal the wounds of societal discrimination. Fifth, employers are not legally competent to develop solely on their own affirmative action plans that grant numerical preferential treatment to whatever groups they perceive as victims of societal discrimination. Finally, in making employment selection decisions, employers need not be totally colorblind if legitimate business interests are served by having a diversified body of employees.

Let us now turn to these areas of common understanding.

Although by no means clear, the Court *appears*, by reason of its discussion in *Bakke* as well as its holdings in other equal employment cases, to take the following positions.

● *Affirmative action under Title VII.* The Supreme Court as a whole appears to be of the view that Title VII does not independently require employers to take affirmative action in order to give employment preference to victims of societal discrimination. The Court previously intimated this view in its seminal decision in *Griggs v. Duke Power*, stating, "The Act [Title VII] does not command that any person be hired simply because he was formerly the subject of discrimination or because he is a member of a minority group." In *Bakke*, Justice Powell referred with approval to this point in the *Griggs* case, and Justice Brennan expressed a similar opinion, saying, "Title VII clearly does not require employers to take action to remedy the disadvantages imposed upon racial minorities by hands other than their own" Justice Brennan argued, however, that while Title VII does not require affirmative action, it also does not prohibit it.

The absence of any independent obligation under Title VII to maintain an affirmative action plan which gives numerical preferences for the hiring of minorities and females was underscored by *Furnco Const. Corp. v. Waters*, a decision handed down by the Court in the week following *Bakke*. In *Furnco*, the company's policy was not to hire walk-on applicants at its gate; as a result, two qualified minority bricklayers who sought employment at the jobsite were not employed. However, there was no finding that the hiring practices were a pretext for racial discrimination. The lower court, holding that the company's refusal to hire at the gate violated Title VII in light of the historic inequality of treatment of black workers and the fact that the company's hiring practice did not maximize employment opportunities for black bricklayers, ruled that the company had to adopt a hiring procedure that not only was job related but also followed the employer to consider the largest number of minority applicants. In reversing, the Supreme Court stated, "Title VII . . . does not impose a duty to adopt a hiring procedure that maximizes hiring of minority employees." Thus, it seems clear from both the *Bakke* debate and the *Furnco* decision that while Title VII clearly demands the elimination of racially discriminatory practices, there is no legal duty to adopt an affirmative action plan giving employment preferences to minority groups and females.

• *Individual rights to equality versus minority group rights to preferential consideration.* The majority of the Supreme Court also appears to be of the view that under Title VII the right of an individual to equal opportunity regardless of race supersedes the interest of minority groups to increase their representation in the work force. In approaching this problem, one should bear in mind the earlier case of *McDonald v. Santa Fe Trail Transp. Co.*, in which the Supreme Court held that Title VII prohibits racial discrimination in private employment against whites on the same grounds as against nonwhites. In so holding, however, the Court emphasized that it did not consider the permissibility of affirmative action programs. Thus, the *Bakke* case represented the first occasion for the Court to discuss whether the Title VII rights of white employees are also protected from discrimination caused by affirmative action for blacks as a group. In *Bakke*, Justice Stevens wrote, "The basic policy of the statute [Title VII] requires that we focus on fairness to individuals rather than fairness to classes." Justice Stevens went on to state that in enacting Title VII, Congress intended that the principle of *individual* equality, without regard to race, was one on which all races had a meeting of the minds. Justice Powell appeared to agree with the Stevens view. In *Bakke*, Justice Powell, again quoting from *Griggs*, noted that "discriminatory preference for any group, minority or majority, is precisely and only what Congress has proscribed."

This point has again been underscored by the Court in its more recent *Furnco* decision. The Court in that case repeated its view that under Title VII the rights of individuals are paramount over the rights of racial groups. In this connection, the *Furnco* court stated: "It is clear beyond cavil that the obligation imposed by Title VII is to provide an equal opportunity for *each* applicant regardless of race, without regard to whether members of the applicant's race are already proportionately represented in the work force." (Emphasis in original.) Thus, the views of the majority, as reinforced by *Furnco*, lead to the conclusion that the Court will not abridge the individual rights of present workers to be free from racial discrimination in order to heal the wounds of past discrimination.

● *Preferential treatment to remedy findings of past discrimination*. The Court appears to recognize one clear exception to the principle that individual rights prevail over minority group interests under Title VII. When a judicial, legislative, or administrative body with competence to act in the EEO area has found unlawful past discrimination, racial or sexual preference may be used as a remedy. The Supreme Court previously expressed this opinion in *Franks v. Bowman Transp. Co.*, where, to remedy past discrimination, an employer was required to give the black victims retroactive seniority even though this adversely affected the seniority expectations of innocent white workers.

Justice Powell declined in his *Bakke* opinion to go beyond *Furnco*. He emphasized that "in the absence of proven constitutional or statutory violations," the Court has not approved preferential racial classifications. He further found that the principles of Title VII supported the proposition that "findings of identified discrimination must precede the fashioning of remedial measures embodying racial classifications." Although the Stevens opinion did not expressly so state, judging from the substance of his opinion as a whole one gets the impression that the Stevens bloc would join Powell on this issue.

Just as the *Bakke* Court struck down under the fourteenth amendment (and inferentially under Title VI) the University of California's racial classifications for admission to medical schools, the Powell view is likely to proscribe racial classifications designed by employers to generally increase minority utilization in their work force when such racial lines are not predicated on findings of past discrimination and result in the rejection of better-qualified white applicants. Moreover, according to Justice Powell, whether such classifications are termed goals or timetables is not determinative. If the classification is "a line drawn on the basis of race and ethnic status," it probably will be considered presumptively unlawful and justifiable only as a necessary scheme to remedy past discrimination.

On the other hand, Justice Brennan, apparently speaking on this issue for a minority of the Court, argued that employers, even in the absence of their own past discrimination, were free under Title VII to adopt affirmative action plans to assist minorities to overcome the obstacles created by past discrimination. He stated that action designed to remedy the disadvantages imposed upon racial minorities was consistent with the remedial goals of Title VII and that past decisions of the Supreme Court under Title VII have supported preferential treatment for those disadvantaged by societal or racial discrimination in order to promote their participation in previously segregated areas of public life. He went on to say that such preferential treatment has not been reserved for those who as individuals have suffered from racial discrimination. According to Justice Brennan, "Such relief does not require as a predicate proof that recipients of preferential advancement have been individually discriminated against; and it is enough that each recipient is within a general class of persons likely to have been the victims of discrimination."

Powell's view that "proven constitutional or statutory violations" must precede the use of preferential or racial classifications must be understood in conjunction with the Court's earlier decision in *United Airlines v. Evans*. United Airlines maintained a policy of refusing to allow its female flight attendants to marry. When Evans married, in 1968, she was forced to resign, but she did not file a charge with the EEOC. In 1972, she was hired as a new employee and was not credited with any seniority from past employment. In the meantime, the no-marriage policy was ruled unlawful under Title VII. Evans filed a lawsuit claiming that the failure to credit her with back seniority perpetuated the unlawful conduct of United Airlines in forcing her to resign because of her marriage. The Supreme Court disagreed. The Court held that because Evans did not file a timely charge of discrimination with regard to her termination, United Airlines was entitled to treat this past discriminatory act as lawful. The Court stated,

> A discriminatory act which is not made the basis for a timely charge is the legal equivalent of a discriminatory act which occurred before the statute was passed . . . [I]t is merely an unfortunate event in history which has *no present legal consequences*.

Combining Justice Powell's views in *Bakke* that there must be a proven statutory violation with the *Evans* case well might lead to the conclusion that acts of past discrimination cannot be the basis for remedial preferential treatment unless such discriminatory acts had been made the basis of a timely charge of discrimination. In other words, an employer's own discriminatory refusal to hire blacks and women in the past might not serve as a predicate for remedial preferential treatment to members of this group if such past discrimination was never made the subject of a timely complaint of discrimination.

• *Voluntary versus required preferential treatment*. Related to the question of whether racial lines can be used to help remedy societal as well as personal discrimination is this issue: Can an employer adopt numerical racial remedies based on its own self-analysis, or must it await findings of discrimination by an administrative, judicial, or legislative body before establishing such remedies? The Court was sharply divided on this issue also. Justice Powell opined that the University of California was not legally competent to make decisions as to whether its past conduct mandated racially designed numerical remedies. Justice Powell contended that in order to establish racial selection lines, the decision-maker must have both the authority and capability of establishing on the record that the racial lines were responsive to identify discrimination. Justice Powell concluded that he was unwilling to convert a remedy reserved for violations of legal rights into "a privilege that all institutions throughout the nation could grant at their pleasure to whatever groups were perceived as victims of societal discrimination."

Justice Brennan took strenuous issue with Justice Powell's restrictions on voluntarily established racial objectives. He argued that Title VII was remedial in nature and that to condition racial remedies on prior government action will bring civil rights progress to a screeching halt. Brennan stated that the public policy stresses the importance of voluntary efforts to assure equal opportunity. The EEOC recently issued guidelines authorizing an employer to voluntarily adopt racial preferences if, based on its own self-analysis, the employer concludes that there is a reasonable basis to believe that the preferences are necessary to remedy previous discrimination. Powell's contrary views leave very much in doubt the wisdom of voluntarily adopting tightly drawn numerical employment objectives based on race or sex in the absence of a formal finding of past discrimination and further questions the vitality of the EEOC's proposed affirmative action guidelines.

• *Preferential treatment under Executive Order 11246*. While the Court's majority appears to espouse the supremacy of individual rights to equal opportunity under Title VII over the minority group interests in obtaining a fair share of the work force, the Court suggested that a different result might obtain when racial lines are drawn pursuant to an employer's obligation under Executive Order 11246 and involve an administrative determination of past discrimination. Justice Brennan traced with approval the history of the Order and its endorsement by the lower courts, the attorney general, and Congress itself. According to Brennan, the use of racial goals by government contractors to increase minority representation does not conflict with Title VII.

Justice Powell, on the other hand, did not go that far. He noted that lower courts have approved affirmative action racial preferences under Executive Order 11246 where a legislative or administrative body has made a determination of past discrimination by particular industries and then fashioned the remedies to rectify the discrimination. *"But,"* he explained, the Supreme Court never has approved preferential classifications in the absence of proving constitutional, statutory violations. By the use of the word *But* Powell appeared to draw a line separating the lower courts' views from his own, and he thus suggested that even under the Executive Order racial and numerical remedies must be predicated on administrative findings of past discrimination. Justice Powell thus, for the time being, appears to have withheld the endorsement even of racial lines drawn pursuant to Executive Order 11246, absent administrative findings of past discrimination.

• *Consideration of race to achieve a legitimate nonracial objective*. The part of the *Bakke* decision magnified by the public is the view of a majority of the Court that race may be taken into account not to draw racial lines but rather to achieve a broader, nonracial objective. Justice Powell said that the University of California could take race into account as one of many factors in order to achieve legitimate educational interests of having a culturally diverse student body. Because employers do not have a comparably compelling interest in assuring a culturally diverse work force, Justice Powell's views as to when race may be taken into account are awkward to apply in an employment context. However, perhaps an employer's interest in providing employees with the benefits of a culturally diverse work force, or proof that diversity will enhance sales, will suffice as a legitimate business interest—in which case Justice Powell and the majority of the Court would not oppose race consciousness.

The signals from the *Bakke* decision indicate that the views of a majority of the Supreme Court do not coincide with all federal policies on equal employment and affirmative action. As presently proposed, the EEOC's Affirmative Action Guidelines encourage employers to conduct a self-analysis to determine whether there is a reasonable basis for concluding that the employer may be held in violation of Title VII and, if so, to establish appropriate solutions— which can include racial and sexual goals, timetables, ratios, and other numerical remedies. The Guidelines promise to find no cause and to dismiss any charges filed by nonminority persons who claim that they were denied equal employment opportunities as a result of the preferential numerical considerations established by the employer. The EEOC should reassess its Guidelines in light of the contrary views of Justice Powell as well as the opinion of Justices Stevens, Rehnquist, Stewart, and Chief Justice Burger that the 1964 Civil Rights Act emphasizes individual rights over group rights. The Guidelines could dangerously mislead employers into believing that the federal government will support racial discrimination against nonminorities and thus encourage breach of the very essence of the equal employment principle.

The OFCCP should also reassess its policies in light of *Bakke*. Existing requirements that government contractors adopt strict yearly goals and timetables, especially where there is no evidence that the contractor engaged in past discrimination, appear to be on a collision course with Justice Powell's views. On the other hand, the many other components of affirmative action planning, including recruitment, analysis of problem areas, and the development of job-related selection criteria, have not been questioned by the *Bakke* Court, and there is no reason to doubt that the OFCCP's basics of affirmative action planning will remain operative.

Going through an
OFCCP Compliance Review

Donald J. Horton

Most of you are familiar with affirmative action programs, Executive Order 11246, and the Office of Federal Contract Compliance Programs (OFCCP). However, some of you probably are unfamiliar with what to expect in the event of a compliance review by the OFCCP. This article will help you cope with the compliance review and give some tips on how to survive unscathed.

What Is a Compliance Review?

The OFCCP is charged under Executive Order 11246 with assuring that federal contractors provide equal employment opportunity. The requirement that covered employers initiate a written affirmative action plan (AAP) is the major tool in promoting this goal. It is hoped that the self-analysis involved in preparing an AAP will make the employer aware of its equal employment deficiencies and will lead to voluntary actions to remedy any problem in that area. However, as we are all aware, the OFCCP does not rely strictly upon voluntary compliance. Compliance reviews periodically are conducted to determine if an employer is striving for the goal of equal opportunity.

Donald J. Horton is with the Houston, Tex., law firm of Andrews, Kurth, Campbell & Jones, and specializes in labor law.

The Steps of a Compliance Review

The steps in a compliance review are:

1. The notification letter
2. The desk audit
3. The on-site review
4. The exit interview
5. The show-cause order

Each step will be discussed below.

The Notification Letter

An employer first discovers that it is going to be reviewed when it receives a letter of notification from the OFCCP. Usually, the first question that pops into the employer's head is, "Why me?" It is important to realize that there is no reason, necessarily, to panic. Compliance reviews are initiated for a number of reasons and the company probably is not being reviewed because of a predetermination that it is a "gross discriminator," but because the firm is in a targeted industry or because the company happened to have been randomly selected for review.

The Desk Audit

The notification letter initiates the second, and very important, step of the review process—the desk audit. The desk audit begins with a request that the contractor's AAP be forwarded to the OFCCP compliance officer. Also, there will be a request for extensive documentation supporting the AAP as well as copies of the company's EEO-1s for the past several years.

Some or all of the following also will be sought:

1. Copies of seniority lists with minorities and women designated
2. Organizational charts
3. Lines of progression
4. Applicant flow information
5. Selection procedures
6. Lists on promotions and transfers identifying minorities and women
7. Terminations by department

8. Participation of minorities and women in training programs
9. Labor agreements
10. Copies of outstanding EEOC charges and of any agreements following charges

It is important to get off on the right foot with the OFCCP. Therefore, I strongly would suggest that every effort be made to meet the deadline for submission of the AAP and supporting documentation. If an extension is needed, ask for it in writing after making an oral appeal. However, it is difficult to get an extension, so you must support your request with substantial reasons.

On the basis of the desk audit, the compliance officer is authorized to determine whether further investigation is necessary or whether the contractor is in compliance. Therefore, it is advisable to make every effort to limit the compliance review process to the desk audit. Toward this end, a letter should be sent accompanying the requested documents, pledging your cooperation and offering any additional documentation or other information that the compliance officer may need to complete his or her investigation. The compliance officer would undoubtedly prefer to complete the review at this stage if possible.

Carefully examine each document and piece of information before sending it to OFCCP. If there is any confidential information, make sure that it is properly coded in case it is disclosed. As an additional precaution, the letter transmitting the requested information to the OFCCP should contain a clause stating that the documents are to be kept confidential and that this is the understanding under which they are being supplied.

The On-Site Review

While you should make every effort to limit the compliance review to the desk-audit stage, it is rare that the OFCCP will not proceed to the next step—the on-site review. Ten days to three weeks notice generally is given before the on-site review begins. This stage should take no longer than a couple of days unless the company is very large or special problems are encountered.

The on-site review could be much broader than the desk audit. The compliance officer can look into things that were never part of the desk audit, so be prepared to have everything available in your affirmative action plan that you said you would. For example, if your affirmative action commitment was to contact employment agencies specializing in minorities, then you should have letters to those agencies.

Two important jobs must be tackled before the on-site review begins—review the AAP and prepare supervisory and management personnel. Carefully review the AAP and make copies of documents that show your positive achievements and demonstrate your accomplishment of goals, timetables, and other affirmative-action objectives. Also, you want to demonstrate to the compliance officer that you are making good faith efforts to achieve your goals and objectives, even though they may not have been reached yet. Therefore, make copies of documents that demonstrate these good faith efforts, such as letters to minority universities and other employment sources and your participation in any kind of special community programs to promote minority recruiting. Remember that the AAP is not a stagnant document; it should be updated and revised when necessary. If changes should be made, provide this information to the compliance officer, either in the desk-audit stage or at the on-site review. Copies of any documents that the reviewer has requested prior to coming on site should be made.

Interviews of Management Personnel

When the compliance officer is on site he or she will want to interview supervisory and management personnel. Therefore, it is important that management personnel be prepared for the review and that they fully understand what it entails. The company must emphasize the positive actions it has taken and the success it has had eliminating any underutilization. Therefore, if possible, all department heads or managers should be briefed before the on-site review so they can project a positive image and emphasize the successes of the department and company.

In addition to briefing supervisors and management personnel about the kinds of questions that may be asked by the review officer, it also is advisable to provide them with a list of questions that may be asked.

When conducting the on-site review, the compliance officer will want to know how the contractor has attempted to establish its EEO image in the community, whether institutional as well as recruitment advertising is used, and whether an EEO reference is used in both.

The officer will want to know which media are used for recruiting, and especially will want to know if the recruiting is oriented toward minorities and women. The officer also will want to know if there are minority and women recruiters. Not only will the compliance officer be interested in the external dissemination of the company's EEO policy, but also he will want to know whether lower level supervisors have received the EEO message. The officer will want to know whether management has made it clear that it will take disciplinary action for failure to adhere to these policies.

Either company counsel or a company representative well versed in EEO matters should be present at all interviews of management personnel. A positive impression will be made if the compliance officer is able to conduct the interview with as little interference as possible. However, company representatives should try to focus on the positive. This can be done by politely refreshing the interviewee's memory or by offering explanations about any problems. This does not mean that the company representative should try to take over the interview or unduly interfere. Rather, the representative should simply interject explanations, information, and raise topics that will jog the interviewee's memory.

Try to make the compliance officer's visit with your company as pleasant as possible so that he or she will be favorably disposed to find compliance. The officer should be treated with the utmost courtesy and respect and should not be left with the impression that the firm does not have the time, or considers the procedure an interference with business, even though that may be the case.

As the old saying goes, "It's the little things that count." Therefore, do those little things to make a favorable impression. For example, provide the compliance officer with directions on how to get to the facility and provide a parking place close to the meeting place. Begin the day with a warm greeting. Do not keep the compliance officer waiting in the reception area more than a few seconds.

The company representative who is most familiar with EEO matters should greet the compliance officer, offer him or her a cup of coffee, and sit down and have a few minutes of pleasant conversation. It also may be wise for one of the company executives to greet the compliance officer and make a positive statement about the company's EEO efforts. Then, get down to business and provide the compliance officer with a pleasant place to work where there is a desk and a telephone. The company representative should be able to give full attention to the compliance review during the next two or three days. Management personnel, while being interviewed, should make every effort to be available without interference from telephone calls and the routine matters of business.

Interviews of Employees

The compliance officer also will wish to speak to employees other than management personnel and to those that he or she considers may have been discriminated against. While it is not mandatory that an interview take place during company time, it is recommended that the firm cooperate and allow interviews of employees on company time and on company premises. The employer's representative has the right to be present when employees are being interviewed, but it is advisable not to be present. If the interview is on company time, the compliance officer always will be cognizant that the employee is away from his or her work station and probably will attempt to keep the interview short. If the employee is interviewed on company time, then the employer's representative will know who it is and may have a general idea about what the employee's complaints or comments might be. Then, an attempt can be made to explain some of the complaints, anticipate some of the problems raised by the interviews, and minimize any adverse comment.

The company representative should take careful notes of all the meetings he or she attends. The notes may be a tip as to the direction the compliance officer is going so that preparations can be made to answer any deficiency charges.

If the compliance officer makes an unreasonable demand for information or documents, then insist that the request be made in writing. This may make the compliance officer back off. If not, the incident may be used later as evidence of the unreasonable demand.

The Exit Interview

The final stage of the on-site review is the exit interview. At this interview, the compliance officer should itemize any deficiencies and seek to get an agreement from the contractor to remedy the deficiencies by a specific date. If questions are asked for which there are no answers at the time, the company representative should agree to do whatever research is necessary and provide the compliance officer with the answer at a later date. Then, the commitment should be lived up to.

When it is obvious that there are deficiencies in the AAP, then admit the errors and demonstrate that the company will act to remedy the deficiencies. The reviewer should be left with the impression that the firm is working with and not against him or her, and that both of you want to insure that affirmative action is working.

However, make no promises to do something that cannot be done within the deadline of your commitment. It may be advisable to agree to remedy some of the deficiencies and incorporate this agreement into a commitment letter. However, it may be best to insist that the compliance officer provide a written listing of *all* deficiencies. When appropriate, a brief should be submitted addressing each of the deficiencies.

After the review is completed, a letter to the reviewing officer should be written, expressing the feeling that the review accomplished some positive results. Thank the officer for his or her cooperation.

The brief is an extremely important document and should address each deficiency and state the points with which the contractor agrees or disagrees. The brief, of course, should attempt to point out in a positive fashion the accomplishments of the contractor and point out any special programs or actions taken.

It also is suggested that a draft letter of commitment be sent along with the brief. The commitment letter should be an honest attempt to resolve the deficiencies that the contractor believes exist. Otherwise, the draft will not be taken seriously, and more stringent commitments may be sought by the OFCCP. Of course, the proposed letter should make it clear that the contractor is entering into the commitment only because it is resolving all deficiencies. The commitment should not be broader than what the contractor really is willing to undertake and should outline the corrective action along with a timetable for such action.

It is recommended that this letter-of-commitment process be pursued because, in a conciliation agreement, it may be difficult to adhere to the recommended language of the OFCCP Compliance Manual.

The Show-Cause Order

If the OFCCP is happy with the company's letter of commitment or a conciliation agreement has been entered into, it will issue notice of compliance. However, if an agreement is not reached, the OFCCP must then either issue a notice of compliance or issue a show-cause notice. If a show-cause notice is issued, the contractor may seek a hearing in accordance with 41 C.F.R. § 60-2.2(b). From this point on the matter should be turned over to counsel.

EMPLOYEE RIGHTS

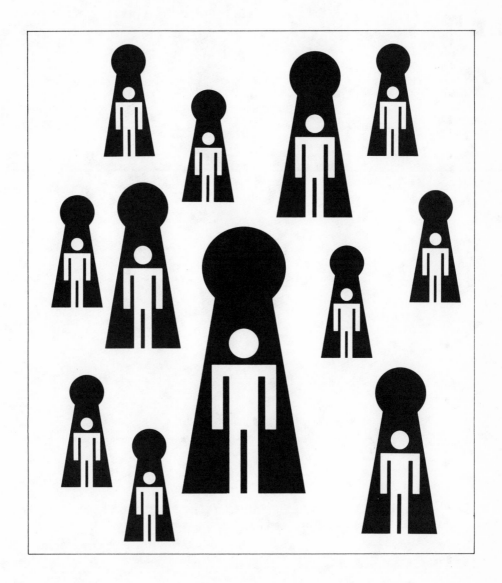

Some In-House
EEO Grievance Procedures
Actually Work!

Craig W. Cole

Disagreements between employers and employees are inevitable. They may involve alleged mistreatment by a supervisor, a dispute over pay or promotion, or a difference of opinion over the propriety of an organizational or company policy. A dispute may have overtones of race, sex, religion, or other factors forbidden by law to influence employment practices. Allegations of discrimination are particularly difficult to handle, because they are highly emotional and frequently difficult to analyze on a strictly issue-oriented basis.

Regardless of the nature of the dispute, unresolved conflict is likely to fester until it erupts into undesirable activity (from the employer's viewpoint): EEO legal action, union grievances, attempts to organize, low productivity, poor morale, or outright sabotage.

For at least these reasons, it is in an employer's interests to provide an internal mechanism that will serve four main purposes:

(1) To bring EEO complaints to the surface;

(2) To allow for examination of complaints;

(3) To diffuse hostility; and

(4) To resolve complaints without outside intervention.

Craig W. Cole is vice president of Brown & Cole, Inc., a retail food operation in Bellingham, Washington. He also is a consultant on EEO matters and is a member of the Washington Governor's Committee on Employment of the Handicapped.

Why Not Use the Traditional Methods for Resolving Complaints?

Many employers question the necessity of an internal complaint-handling procedure for EEO cases (and similar disputes) when other mechanisms for such purposes are already in place. The existing avenues of redress typically take one of three forms:

(1) A grievance procedure established by collective bargaining agreement which may involve a formal arbitration hearing;

(2) A company policy that encourages employees to pursue grievances through the chain of command, starting with their supervisors; or

(3) The right to file a complaint with government agencies.

However, none of these approaches to problem solving is particularly advantageous to the employer.

The union grievance and government complaint procedures share a common fault: they are based on assumptions that the employer is unwilling to resolve disputes on its own and that the parties will be unable to "work things out" together. They ultimately result in an imposed resolution, which is likely to cause lingering hostility between the "winner" and the "loser." Additionally, union grievance and government complaint processes are highly formal and uncomfortable methods for all parties, so they are often used only after there is little hope for an amicable settlement. They require people to choose sides, to become adversaries. Accordingly, they make it difficult for people to work with one another during and after the process. They may resolve *legal* questions, but they do little to improve the interpersonal relationships of the parties.

Reliance on union grievance procedures can reinforce the notion that only the union protects the employee from whims of the employer. Moreover, there is some question whether union personnel and the union grievance process have the expertise and sensitivity to effectively handle problems of discrimination. In fact, unions are frequently seen as either active or silent partners with employers in committing alleged discrimination, through the negotiation of discriminatory labor agreements, by their own history of discrimination, or by acquiescence.

Government investigations, while appearing to be a more promising avenue of redress to the employee, can lead to legal action far exceeding in scope the original complaint. It is not uncommon for an individual's complaint to serve as the catalyst for class action litigation or for placing government contracts in jeopardy.

The "see your supervisor" approach to dispute resolution is frequently unused because he or she is often the source of the problem. The approach relies on enlightened supervisors who are able to look at problems (perhaps criticism) objectively and react fairly and even magnanimously. Further, employees and their supervisors consider "going over the supervisor's head" (to upper management) to be distasteful.

Thus, traditional methods for handling EEO complaints fail to produce results acceptable to both parties: the methods are either too formal and devoid of good faith compromise (the union grievance and government complaint approaches), or they are too informal and reliant upon the charity of the supervisor, leaving little real protection for the aggrieved employee (as with the "see your supervisor" approach). And none of these approaches adequately addresses the interpersonal problems associated with resolution of a discrimination complaint.

Though an employer cannot prevent a person from going to outside organizations to seek help, it can provide a flexible in-house alternative for the review of problems. This would encourage the parties themselves to develop a workable solution to the dispute.

Case Examples

The arguments in favor of internal EEO complaint procedures are not just theoretical—successful procedures have been operating for years.

The Boeing Company, a multistate employer, has encouraged its employees to raise complaints internally since 1968. Over 25 percent of employee discrimination complaints are resolved internally, says John A. Priest, corporate EEO administrator. Grievants are asked to bring problems to their supervisors, personnel officers, or anyone else with whom they feel comfortable. The complaints are forwarded to the appropriate work unit EEO administrator, who investigates the charges. (Supervisors are also encouraged to notify the EEO staff whenever they become aware of potential problems.) The EEO administrator develops a written finding on the allegation, including a recommendation for appropriate remedies. The report is reviewed by the corporate EEO office and then transmitted to departmental management, which, according to Priest, usually accepts the recommendation of his office.

The biggest asset of the procedure, says Priest, is that it allows for the *prompt* settlement of a problem, before it becomes too big or too heated to resolve, "There is almost nothing worse than just letting one of these cases sit," he adds.

Seattle First National Bank instituted an "Internal Discrimination Inquiry Procedure" three years ago for its 7,600 employees. Employees are asked to discuss their complaints with their supervisors first, and to contact the Affirmative Action Section if they are not satisfied. An affirmative action officer then conducts an investigation "just like an enforcement agency" and recommends remedial action, according to Sandra Sullivan, assistant vice president with the Affirmative Action Section. If the complainant disagrees with the recommendation, he or she may take the complaint to a three-member "appeal hearing panel," consisting of two people within the bank and an EEO professional outside the organization. The panel hears from the complainant, the defending work unit, and the affirmative action staff. It then renders a decision that is binding on the bank.

Sullivan reports that of twenty-four internal complaints processed by the bank, one-fourth have resulted in a remedy for the complainant. More important, only two cases resulted in intervention by outside parties. In all other cases, the complainants agreed with, or at least accepted, the internal adjudications.

"We look at it as a very cost-saving procedure—a very efficient method for getting complaints resolved," comments Sullivan. "Some of the complaints weren't huge ones to us. But they were to the people complaining."

Internal complaint mechanisms not only bring problems to the surface, they also help avoid inquiries by outside bodies. One of Honolulu-based Dillingham Maritime's companies received a telephone call from the U.S. Equal Employment Opportunity Commission (EEOC) about an employee who believed that her working conditions were adversely affected by her race. Before initiating formal complaint action, the employee had asked the EEOC to attempt an informal resolution.

David B. Ballash, the company's president, asked the EEOC for a chance to settle the matter through a newly developed internal complaint procedure. The Commission agreed, and Ballash directed the EEO officer to mediate the dispute between the complainant and her supervisors. A successful resolution prevented the filing of a charge with the government and consequent investigation. Following this incident, the company was similarly able to resolve a case that was again at the doorstep of an enforcement agency. Neither settlement involved the expenses of back pay, attorneys' fees, and great expenditures of time, which frequently result from settlements instigated by a government agency.

Guiding Principles

An employer's "attitude" will greatly influence the success of an internal complaint procedure. The Washington State Human Rights Commission has published guidelines suggesting the following policies for employers:

(1) That internal complaints are encouraged as being in the best interests of the employer;

(2) That each complaint will be examined expeditiously, thoroughly, honestly, and impartially to determine its merit;

(3) That problems found to exist will be immediately corrected and remedied according to applicable laws, regulations, guidelines, and legal concepts;

(4) That the internal grievance process will be flexible and must allow for good faith negotiation between the parties toward a mutually acceptable solution;

(5) That no retaliation or discrimination of any form will occur against a person for making a complaint.

[*Guidelines for Handling Internal Discrimination Complaints*, Washington State Human Rights Commission, November 13, 1975; 1 Washington Human Rights Reporter SG-17.]

An employer should add one more tenet: That the supervisor's traditional authority will not be threatened, except when his or her actions have been unfair or unlawful.

This last tenet highlights the traditional dilemma in dispute handling. The process must be used to demonstrate the employer's willingness to correct wrongdoing. At the same time, it should be emphasized that the supervisor's judgment will prevail, unless he or she has committed unfair or unlawful actions. How this tightrope can be walked will be discussed later in this article.

Two Ways to Structure an Internal Resolution Process

As the case examples discussed earlier in this article illustrate, there are two common approaches to developing internal complaint resolution processes: the "appeals committee" approach and the "management intervention" approach.

Appeals Committee Approach

The appeals committee approach usually involves a representative committee of management and nonmanagement people, as well as a sex/ethnic balance. Grievants are commonly required to seek a solution to their problems through the supervisory chain before bringing the matter to the appeals committee. The complaint is usually reduced to writing, with the "defending" department or supervisor providing a written response to the charge. A hearing is held, with both sides in attendance, accompanied by supporting witnesses and documents. Sometimes an attorney or another employee is permitted to act as an advocate for the grievant. The committee hears the differing viewpoints, evaluates the evidence, and renders a decision, which is either advisory or binding, subject to review by top management.

An advantage of this approach is its democratic appearance, which lends credibility to the process and fosters acceptance of its decisions as being fair and reasonable. It puts several minds to work on solving difficult problems, and, because it involves group action, makes it easier to render decisions that are controversial or unpleasant to management.

The appeals committee process also has inherent disadvantages. It is sometimes unwieldy and slow to react to problems that need quick attention. The committee can become uncontrollable, creating more problems than solutions, forcing management to overrule its decisions, thereby undercutting the credibility of the process. It is difficult to educate an entire committee on the fine points of law so that it can make intelligent decisions, and the committee can become a forum for theatrics and the airing of dirty laundry. Even when a decision is favorable to the grievant, the company seldom gets credit for dealing with problems in good faith—after all, it was the committee that did it. Finally, appeals committees tend to be structured and formal. They usually impose resolutions without addressing the underlying defects in interpersonal relationships.

Because appeals committees are somewhat like courts of law, they have credibility and a certain democratic charm. But because they are like courts, they also force people to become adversaries, to choose up sides and fight it out on a carefully structured (and formal) battleground. Many potential grievants will be scared off by this formality and openness. Others will thrive on it—if they don't find it so similar to outside legal remedies that they might as well skip the internal process and use the real thing: government enforcement agencies or the courts.

Management Intervention Approach

Some managers detest the committee approach to resolving individual complaints. They believe that "good management" means cleaning up your own house—you don't need a committee to do it for you. And based on experience with labor-management committees on safety and other matters, they fear that committees will become politicized and uncontrollable. These managers prefer the management intervention approach to structuring an internal grievance process.

"Management intervention" is based on the premise that the company is best protected by regulating itself through management action. The process is usually simple: if a person cannot resolve his or her differences within the supervisory chain, the employee is encouraged to get in touch with a personnel manager or an EEO officer. It then becomes this individual's obligation to look into the facts of the dispute and to either recommend a decision to higher authorities or to mediate the dispute between the parties.

To be effective and to have the cooperation of all company personnel, the management intervenor should be under the direct authority of the chief executive officer (CEO), thus becoming a kind of troubleshooter for top management. The emphasis should be placed on working out a solution acceptable to both sides—in fact, to get the sides working *together* toward a solution. The intervenor is generally someone who is viewed as "neutral," either a personnel or EEO officer, or, in smaller companies, a top manager. Some companies have entertained the possibility of borrowing a skilled intervenor from another organization, especially in highly controversial cases.

There are many ways to mediate disputes, but typically an intervenor will interview both sides of the dispute individually, to define the conflict, establish the ground rules for using the process, solicit suggested remedies, and move the parties toward a better understanding of one another's point of view. Eventually, the parties are brought together with the intervenor to begin working out a solution.

Ideally, the intervenor serves as a catalyst for resolution but is eventually able to extricate himself or herself from the proceedings, allowing the conflicting sides to conclude a solution on their own. If no solution is reached, the intervenor's recommendation is passed on to top management for review and determination.

The advantages of this approach are many. Management can maintain control of the situation and take quick action in response to problems. The process becomes a tool for management to remain informed of problem areas and liabilities within the organization, and it is not likely to cause a public airing of grievances. It is flexible and informal, requiring few well-trained staff members to make it work. A skilled intervenor can work with the parties individually, nudging them toward a mutually acceptable solution that improves the interpersonal relationships as well as resolves the immediate source of conflict.

The management intervention approach is less likely perceived as a threat to the supervisor's authority, since it clearly is a management-owned and operated procedure. At the same time, it reaffirms top management's demand that supervisors operate in a fair and nondiscriminatory manner. And, finally, when a problem is resolved, management gets the credit.

A major disadvantage of the management intervention process is that it relies too heavily on the effectiveness of a single person, who may come under pressure to "cover up" or to talk the grievant out of his or her claim; also, the intervenor may be intimidated by senior managers. It is easy for either side to condemn the intervenor's recommendations as being the arbitrary or biased actions of one person, thus possibly adding an additional personality conflict to the dispute.

For the management intervention approach to be effective, management must have confidence in the problem-solving abilities of its EEO staff, and must be willing to stand behind the intervenor's recommendations. Many EEO officers don't deserve this confidence, and many CEOs are too timid to deal with controversial disputes involving alleged discrimination, particularly when it requires stepping on the toes of a senior manager. Further, this approach doesn't have the charm to the work force that an appeals committee has. Its credibility must come from its demonstrated effectiveness, not from its appearance.

Selecting the Right Approach

Whether it be the appeals committee approach, the management intervention approach, or a hybrid of the two, an internal grievance procedure for EEO matters must be fashioned to fit a particular organization. The major considerations in selecting an approach are as follows:

Staff Expertise. The management intervention approach requires an EEO or personnel staff well trained in law *and* highly skilled in mediating disputes. It takes more than a law degree to bring conflicting sides to accept a compromise solution, or even an adverse determination—and feel that it is reasonable. Indeed, an overly legalistic style in the mediation of internal grievances can produce hostility and a feeling of distrust toward the process.

If a company's EEO or personnel staff lacks either technical knowledge or "people skills," then the appeals committee approach, with its democratic appearance and form, is more likely to be effective.

Executive Commitment. The management intervention approach requires chief executives who have a strong commitment to EEO and who are willing to take action to force, when necessary, a case resolution on an offending department. Many CEOs would rather neglect their EEO responsibilities than tangle with department managers, whose enthusiasm is necessary to make the organization run smoothly and profitably. The appeals committee approach is best suited to this type of management, because it seldom requires the making of tough decisions by top executives. The management intervention approach will probably be more effective, however, under enlightened, strong chief executives.

Preparing the Implementation

Once the approach has been selected, a few preliminary steps should be taken to get the process rolling:

Train the Staff. Before the ribbon is cut on a new internal grievance procedure, the management intervenors or the members of the appeals committee must be trained in EEO law and in investigation and mediation techniques. Potential sources for this training are advertised seminars, a consultant or lawyer that specializes in EEO matters, or even an EEO enforcement agency. Some enforcement agencies (federal, state, or local) will send a representative to your organization to conduct the training. Better yet, if they are convinced of your good intentions, a few enforcement agencies will permit attendance at their in-house sessions for beginning investigators.

Reassure Supervisors. Supervisors and line managers may view an internal grievance procedure as a threat to their authority. Before the procedure is implemented, meetings should be held to inform them of the purpose of the program. Perhaps the most convincing argument is that company-conducted inquiries into problems are much less likely to produce disruption than are those conducted by outside authorities. Further, the process may help many supervisors to find out where conflict exists in the work unit, such conflicts usually having a negative impact on productivity.

The supervisors should be told that their decisions and judgments will be altered only if they are unfair, unlawful, or discriminatory. Finally, the company's policy of nonretaliation (by anyone) for raising a grievance should be reiterated.

Orchestrate Publicity. Publishing the grievance procedure in a policy handbook is not enough. It should be marketed as a product that the organization is offering its employees. It should be included in employee handbooks and in company publications, posted on bulletin boards, summarized in a "stuffer" for pay envelopes, and mentioned at employee meetings. Publicity should be repeated periodically. Be candid about expressing the view that the company is more likely to take a compromising attitude toward claims filed internally, where adversary proceedings are unnecessary. Word-of-mouth publicity is the best sales point. If those who use the process believe it is fair and effective, they will spread the word.

Avoid Defensiveness. The best internal grievance procedure "on paper" can be destroyed by a poor attitude on the part of its administrators or line supervisors and managers. Avoid appearing defensive, above all. This will simply confirm suspicions that the process is a management "whitewash" program.

Conclusion

Some managers view internal grievance procedures for EEO matters as mere exercises in self-flagellation. They believe that encouraging employees to air their complaints will cause more problems than would occur by ignoring the sources of conflict. Fortunately, most managers recognize that unaired grievances frequently cause serious productivity and morale problems. And most important, they know that lack of recourse within an organization forces people to seek remedies outside . . . and that's when the real trouble begins.

Internal EEO grievance procedures will not prevent all disenchanted employees from taking their complaints to the government or the courts. But properly structured internal procedures will allow organizations to demonstrate their goodwill to employees who still believe that their employers can be fair.

Employee Access
to Personnel Files—
The Rising Tide

John C. Fox and Paul J. Ostling

With the belated discovery of federal and state Freedom of Information Acts, the country is undertaking a widespread discussion of "sunshine" and "access" issues. No longer, however, are only public employers affected by the access statutes. Of late, access fever has spilled over into the private sector and has led four state legislatures to require employers to provide employees with access to their personnel files. Several other state legislatures are now contemplating similar statutes.

Recognizing that many corporations, like the government, often maintain great storehouses of information on file, unions and the federal government itself are increasingly trying to find ways to tap into company files. Unaccustomed to outside perusal of corporate records, many managers have recently been startled to discover that they have

John C. Fox is an attorney in the Washington, D.C., office of Pepper, Hamilton & Scheetz. He advises employers in privacy matters.

Paul J. Ostling is assistant general counsel of Arthur Young & Co., New York City.

an obligation to disclose certain kinds of corporate personnel files. This realization, along with the everyday pressures to minimize filing space costs, has led many companies to review their record retention policies and to design programs to discard out-of-date or unneeded records.

Against this background, recent developments in the law regarding access to personnel files by employees, unions, and the government are discussed below along with a very general review of some basic record-keeping requirements imposed by federal law.

Statutes on Employee Access

Currently, there is no federal requirement that employers provide employees with access to their personnel files. Four states, however, have passed statutes giving employees the right to examine their file. These four states are California (Cal. Labor Code §1198.5 (1976)), Oregon (Ore. Ch. 861, L. 1977, effective Jan. 1, 1978), Maine (Maine Rev. Stat. Ann. Tit. 5, Sec. 638, Tit. 30, Sec. 64 and 2257), and Michigan (Mich. Stat. Ann. §1121, as enacted by Ch. 379, L. 1978, effective Jan. 1, 1979).

Michigan's statute is by far the most comprehensive and onerous to management. It provides employees with the right to:

(1) gain access to the records in their personnel file "reasonably near" the employee's place of employment during normal business hours;

(2) challenge inaccuracies in the file and submit to the file a written clarifying statement not to exceed five 8-½" by 11" sheets if the employer refuses to make the requested correction. The employer must disclose the clarifying statement to third parties when the material is released;

(3) compel employer compliance with the Act through an action for actual damages and costs in the circuit court. In addition, employees may recover reasonable attorney's fees and $200 plus costs for a willful and knowing violation.

On the other hand, employers may charge employees for the actual cost to reproduce records, although it is not clear that copying is required, and may maintain a separate investigation file if the company believes the employee is engaged in "criminal activity" that may result in loss or damage to the employer's property. However, the employer must notify the employee about the investigation upon its completion or after two years, whichever comes first. In addition, if no disciplinary action is taken, the investigative file must be destroyed. The Act requires employers to notify employees by first-class mail on or before the day the employer releases a disciplinary report, letter of reprimand, or other disciplinary action to a third party. However, an employer does not need to provide the notice if:

(1) the employee has specifically waived written notice as part of a written, signed employment application with another employer;
(2) the disclosure is ordered in a legal action or arbitration; or
(3) if the information is requested by a government agency as a result of a complaint filed by an employee.

In addition, except when the release is ordered in a legal action or arbitration, an employer must review a personnel record and *delete* all disciplinary reports, letters of reprimand, or other records of disciplinary action *which are more than four years old*.

In contrast to the Michigan statute, California, Maine, and Oregon have short and simple laws. All three states require that employers allow employees access to their personnel file at their place of employment. California does not provide for access to letters of reference. Similarly, Oregon does not require access to confidential records from previous employers. Maine, on the other hand, defines personnel records so broadly that employee evaluations, reports of character, credit reports, and information concerning work habits and compensation appear to be accessible to personnel. In addition, California, like Michigan, does not provide access to investigatory records relating to possible criminal offenses. Unlike the Michigan statute, however, the California law omits additional requirements to either inform the employee or destroy the records upon completion of the investigation.

Numerous states also have Fair Credit Reporting Acts that require employers to obtain the permission of employees before they commence credit checking activities. An exhaustive review of these statutes is not possible here, although company managers should be aware that there are restrictions on the use of credit checking information and on the distribution of such information without prior notification to employees.

The four state statutes, as well as most labor contracts, do not address the issue of union access to employee personnel files. Unions do, however, have an affirmative access right under federal labor laws in grievance hearings.

Privacy Commission Recommendations

The federal government has also given some thought to the idea of regulating private sector personnel record policies. In the Final Report of the Privacy Protection Study Commission released in July 1977, the commission stopped short of recommending that federal legislation be drafted to regulate the private sector. The commission did, however, establish voluntary guidelines for private companies. Among the many recommendations, the commission urged companies to:

- limit the collection of information on employees and applicants to what is relevant to specific decisions;
- give employees access to their personnel records upon request and the right to copy them;
- inform employees and applicants about the uses to which their records are (or will be) put;
- designate and separate those records not available to an employee, although the commission expressed a strong preference for few such records. The commission specifically suggested that individual employment performance, medical, and insurance records be available to employees;
- correct records the employee identifies as inaccurate or explain why corrections were not made;
- curb the release of information to outside requesters without the employee's consent, except for routine directory information concerning position held, employment dates, and salary;
- limit the internal use of records maintained on employees and applicants.

Following the Privacy Commission recommendations, many companies should be undertaking reviews of their personnel practices and overhauling their personnel file systems. Although there is no "model" system, a variety of major companies are now implementing the Privacy Commission voluntary guidelines. In particular, many companies now give employees access and allow them to copy most of their records. Many companies, however, are not making available performance reviews, management succession, or "fast mover" files. Several companies have also established in-house appeals procedures that employees may invoke if the company refuses to delete or revise information challenged as inaccurate. Increasingly, too, companies are requiring *written* requests for information about employees. Also growing is the practice where companies ask employees to sign waivers before the company releases employee data to outside agencies, particularly where the information appears to be of a sensitive nature.

A comprehensive system that observes the requirements and implications of the privacy, access, and EEO laws, would seemingly include the following:

(1) an employment application that includes a waiver authorizing the employer to disclose the contents of the employee's file to those whom the employee grants access (i.e., reference checks by subsequent employers), and to make a credit check where applicable;

(2) separation of employee records into sections—a confidential section containing employer investigations of the employee as permitted by law; an administrative section containing materials unrelated to the employee's performance (i.e., group health coverage and claims, salary authorization numbers, company property assignments receipts, etc.); and, a third section containing information on the employee's performance and advancement;

(3) permission for the employee to review and make notes on those portions of the file which law permits (to protect the company's interests, records should be kept indicating when and where such employee reviews took place);

(4) restriction on access to information contained within employee files to those with a "need to know" within the company and to those who are authorized outside the company (e.g., law enforcement officials, and prospective employers); and,

(5) an aggressive record retention policy that conforms to applicable law.

Release of performance reviews continues to be a particularly sticky issue for many companies. Although several major corporations show employees their reviews on the theory that an employee should know his or her deficiencies in order to improve performance, and on the theory that a performance review that is signed or reviewed by the subject employee cannot later be claimed to be bogus should some EEO or labor litigation arise, most companies do not, fearing adverse morale problems and reduced productivity. In a recent reverse Freedom of Information case in the District of Columbia, for example, several industrial psychologists testified that release of company promotion plans would cause morale and productivity to deteriorate and require managers to devote more time and energy to employee counseling.

A company proposing to disclose its performance reviews must also assess the way in which its managers and supervisors will react. In many cases, companies may find that managers who perform open performance evaluations will mark unsatisfactory workers as satisfactory rather than face a confrontation with an unhappy employee. The company must further assess its litigation posture if employees are repeatedly evaluated as satisfactory by their supervisors and then terminated. This tendency must be thwarted or else the company will create records that contradict its later employment decisions. This is not an uncommon occurrence which company attorneys are then required to explain away in subsequent grievance hearings or legal challenges brought to termination actions.

Government Access to Personnel Files

The federal government has recently been successful in forcing E.I. DuPont de Nemours and Company to disclose employee medical files to it, but not to other members of the public, despite the protests of over six hundred employees who refused to consent to the release.

The National Institute of Occupational Safety and Health (NIOSH), a research office within the Department of Health, Education and Welfare, sought the documents to perform a health hazard evaluation study. DuPont had voluntarily compiled the records for some forty years and used them exclusively for in-house studies. Although DuPont was willing to disclose the records with the names of employees deleted to protect their privacy interests, NIOSH was unwilling to accept the records altered in any way. DuPont, on the other hand, refused to disclose the records with the names of employees included unless the employee gave his or her consent to release.

NIOSH subsequently issued an administrative subpoena to DuPont requiring it to disclose the documents. When 631 employees specifically withheld their consent to the release of their records, DuPont went to federal court in West Virginia seeking a declaratory judgment.

In December 1977, the court upheld NIOSH's position and ordered DuPont to disclose the records on the condition that the government make no subsequent disclosure to the public. Limiting the disclosure to government investigators only and not to the public, the court reasoned, was not a "public" revelation and therefore could not violate anyone's right of privacy.

A similar case was recently decided by a federal district court in Ohio involving General Motors Corporation. As in the *DuPont* case, General Motors asked the court to decide whether the company had an obligation to release employee medical files to NIOSH or whether to refuse government requests for them on employee privacy grounds. In the company's view, it is on the horns of a dilemma: caught on the one hand by the company's obligation to protect the privacy rights of its employees and yet legally bound to respond to government investigations of the company and its employees.

The court avoided the dilemma in October 1978 by ordering General Motors to turn over the medical files to NIOSH but without the names of employees attached if the employees objected. The court gave NIOSH the right, however, to request a listing of employees from General Motors so that it could contact all employees directly and ask for their medical records. The court also gave the affected employees the right to be heard in court concerning the release of their medical records without their consent. Thus, the question whether NIOSH has the right to subpoena the company and its employees over their objection, and to compel either or both parties to supply medical records identified by employee name, was not decided.

The problems faced by General Motors and DuPont are particularly interesting in light of the Privacy Protection Study Commission recommendations, which encouraged the private sector to develop personnel practices that protect the privacy of employee records. The commission stopped short of recommending that legislation be developed applicable to the private sector because it wanted to find out whether private industry could regulate itself. The challenge was thus set for company personnel managers to either do a good job of protecting employee privacy rights or face further legislation mandating it.

Ironically, when DuPont first asked for judicial resolution of its NIOSH subpoena, many government observers were suspicious of what appeared to them to be the self-serving nature of the company's objection. Despite the Privacy Commission mandate, some observers felt that DuPont was attempting to duck the NIOSH investigation by hiding behind the privacy issue. This ignores the fact, however, that DuPont had offered to give government investigators the medical records they sought but with the employee names deleted. The government refused this offer.

The Pending OSHA Access Rule

The *General Motors* and *DuPont* cases signal only the start of a major new push by the Occupational Safety and Health Administration (OSHA) to gain access to employee medical records contained in company personnel files.

OSHA is currently attempting to expand employee access to employer occupational safety and health-related information in what OSHA describes as an effort to make it easier for workplace hazards to be identified, and for work and personal hygiene practices to be followed.

OSHA has issued proposed rules (46 Fed. Reg. 3171-74, July 21, 1978) that would require employers to preserve toxic exposure and medical records of employees, and to allow both present and former employees access to the records.

A "record" under the proposed rules is any recorded information concerning employee exposure to toxic substances or harmful physical agents, whether recorded for occupational health purposes or for other purposes, which an employer makes, maintains, or has access to. Both individual exposure records and general research and statistical studies are included in the scope of the definition.

Employers would be required to preserve such records during an individual's period of employment and for five years after termination of employment, unless specific regulations require a different retention period. An employer would also be required to provide access to the records to the affected workers and their representatives, and to representatives of OSHA and NIOSH.

OSHA has said that the proposed rules do not require the creation of new records, nor any independent responsibility of employers to follow or measure employee exposures. The proposed rules do not set up mandatory requirements on exposure or medical records or determine their format.

OSHA has also issued an interim rule effective July 19, 1978, requiring employers to preserve the records in accordance with the proposed rules until the rule-making process is complete. Hearings on the proposed rules were held in December in Washington, D.C., Chicago, and San Francisco. Until such time as the final rules are adopted, however, employers are not required to provide employees with access to the records.

In addition, OSHA has issued final rules (46 Fed. Reg. 3124-29, July 21, 1978) which allow employees access to "The Log and Summary of Occupational Injuries and Illnesses." Employers of eleven or more persons are required to maintain the log, which covers job-related injuries and illnesses at the workplace. Prior to the new rule, employees only had access to an annual statistical summary of the log.

Record-keeping Requirements

With the growing emphasis on access to information and the spiraling costs to retain files or computerize data, increasing attention needs to be paid to record retention policies. Currently, federal regulations alone present companies with a lengthy, ponderous, and confusing array of record-keeping requirements.

Recognizing this, the Equal Employment Opportunity Commission has recently proposed new equal employment record-keeping requirements that would establish a uniform two-year record retention policy.

A comprehensive review of the numerous major federal record re-

SUMMARY OF RECORD-KEEPING REQUIREMENTS

Records to Be Retained	Period of Retention	Source
Applications for positions known by applicant to be temporary	90 days	ADEA (Age Discrimination in Employment Act)
Records relating to employee terminations	* 6 months	Title VII (1964 Civil Rights Act)
Complaints by Vietnam Era veterans and disabled veterans	1 year	Vietnam Era Veterans Readjustment Assistance Act
Complaints by handicapped employees	1 year	Vocational Rehabilitation Act
All records necessary to complete Form EEO-2 (Apprenticeship)	* 1-2 years	Title VII
Supplementary wage and hour records	2 years	FLSA (Fair Labor Standards Act)
Chronological list of applicants to actual application of individuals for apprenticeship program	2 years	Title VII
Test papers and other records relating to apprenticeship programs	2 years	Title VII
Supplementary wage and hour records	2 years	Walsh-Healy
Specific wage and hour data	3 years	FLSA
Basic personnel and wage and hour information	3 years	ADEA Walsh-Healy
OSHA records	5 years	OSHA
Basic personnel and wage and hour data	5 years	National Apprenticeship Act & Davis-Bacon Act
Labor-Management reports documentation	5 years	(LMRDA) Labor Management Reporting and Disclosure Act

* Proposed change to 2 years

tention periods and requirements is beyond the scope of this article; the table on page 339, however, sets out a variety of common record-keeping requirements faced by most major companies today. A much more detailed, but now somewhat out of date listing, appeared in the *Federal Register*, Volume 39, No. 56, March 21, 1974, entitled "Guide to Record Retention Requirements."

Conclusion

It is apparent that employers have been placed amid a maze of somewhat contradictory policies which underpin the various record-keeping, disclosure and privacy statutes, and decisional law. On the one hand, record-keeping requirements require information gathering, while on the other hand, privacy and consumer credit laws restrict that process. Similarly, while privacy requirements seek to protect confidential employee information, disclosure statutes and case law require access. Moreover, federal record-keeping laws alone are a complicated and tangled mass of requirements.

BENEFITS

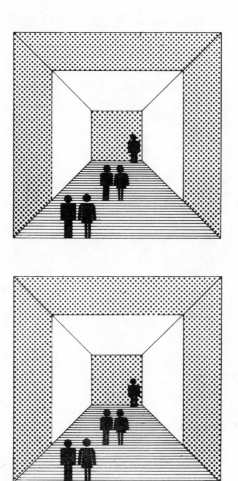

Manhart and Employee Benefit Plans: Confusing the Sex Bias Issue

Joseph R. Rackman

In 1978, the Supreme Court decided two cases of considerable interest for the EEO practitioner. One case received widespread publicity, even though its result could not affect most Americans. The other case received scant publicity, yet it will affect the vast majority of all Americans. One case is well known—the *Bakke* case—which dealt with the problems of reverse discrimination and quotas that favor minority groups to make amends for past wrongs. The other case, lesser known, dealt with sex discrimination in pension plans—the *Manhart* case; it has important implications for all men and women covered by any pension, profit-sharing, life insurance, disability, or health benefit plan sponsored by an employer.

In both cases, the Supreme Court failed to clarify what precise standards should be used in similar cases in the future. Today, no one is certain about what are the limits of permissible reverse discrimination or what constitutes sex discrimination in pension and other employee benefit plans.

This article will analyze the *Manhart* case and explain its broad implications. It will also discuss lawsuits that could be brought by aggrieved males and females. As will be seen, half of all those covered by a company pension or profit-sharing plan may have a well-

Joseph Rackman is with the New York law firm of Weil, Gotshal & Manges, where his practice concentrates on employee benefit plans and tax law.

grounded claim for damages, depending on how the *Manhart* case is finally interpreted.

Facts

Manhart involved a pension plan sponsored and administered by the city of Los Angeles. Both the employer and employees contributed money to the program. City officials determined, based on a study of mortality tables, that its female employees would, as a group, outlive its male employees. Accordingly, the city required the female employees to make significantly larger pension fund contributions than did the males. The result was that female employees took home less pay than male employees. For example, each male and female employee earning $10,000 annually contributed monthly payments of, respectively, $22 and $25. However, on retirement, each employee received the same monthly benefit.

Five female plan participants sued the city, and argued that requiring greater plan contributions from them than from similarly situated males constituted a form of sex discrimination under Title VII of the Civil Rights Act of 1964. That statute makes it unlawful for employers "to discriminate against any individual with respect to his compensation, terms, conditions, or privileges of employment, because of such individual's race, color, religion, sex, or national origin."

A majority of the Supreme Court agreed with the plaintiffs and focused on the Title VII prohibition that bars discrimination against any individual on the basis of sex. The Court acknowledged that women, as a class, live longer than men and that, as a result, greater funds would be required to pay women pension benefits equal to those of similarly situated men. However, the Court reasoned, not all females outlive all males, and while contributions were being collected from employees, the plan's sponsor (the city of Los Angeles) could not know which individual women would predecease the "average woman." Thus, certain individual women would die relatively young, having made greater contributions to the plan than equally situated men, and would not have recouped the benefit of their "excess" plan contributions during retirement. Indeed, the life expectancy of five out of six females is not greater than that of the "average male." In effect, the justification for greater contributions from these particular five out of six individual women would have proven false because of their relatively early deaths. Because of this possibility, the Supreme Court rejected the requirement that all females make greater contributions to the plan.

The situation in *Manhart* is different from the situation where one tests prospective employees to ascertain their qualifications for a given job, even if the tests result in the hiring of few females. For example, a company cannot refuse to hire women as telephone switchmen merely because "average women" lack the necessary physical stamina; however, it will be permitted to require job applicants to pass certain physical tests. In such a situation, each individual applicant is given a chance to qualify for the job, and those discriminated against will be those lacking physical stamina, not women as a class. However, discrimination based on actuarial projections about life expectancy, such as occurred in *Manhart*, even though they are valid, does not justify discrimination against a particular female *individual*, because the statistics do not necessarily correlate to what will be, in fact, that individual woman's life expectancy.

In sum, the Supreme Court decided that the women could not be required to make greater contributions to the plan than similarly situated men. However, the women who initiated the lawsuit did not receive the restitution they requested. They had sued for a refund of their excess contributions to the plan. The Supreme Court denied their demand for several reasons, the most important being the realization that such a decision would affect numerous insurance companies and pension plans and millions of Americans. Indeed, if retroactive relief were readily granted to compensate for sex discrimination in pension plan cases, many large corporations could fall into serious financial difficulty or even bankruptcy.

Implications of *Manhart*

What frightening implications does *Manhart* hold? How does this decision affect numerous insurance companies and pension plans and millions of Americans? After all, the *Manhart* decision dealt only with a pension plan that required unequal contributions from male and female employees. Very few pension plans in the United States require such unequal contributions. What, then, are the hidden terrors of *Manhart*? These can best be illustrated by example.

Suppose a man and woman, both age 65, have participated in their company's profit-sharing plan and are now retiring. Each year the company has set aside for the man and woman 15 percent of their salary in individual accounts. These annual contributions and their earnings over the years now total $100,000 each for the man and woman. Now that they are retiring, the male and female employee have a choice: they can each take their $100,000 in one lump sum, or they can receive an annuity payable for their lifetime. Utilizing annuity tables, the man is entitled, in lieu of his $100,000 lump sum benefit, to a retirement benefit of $1,000 a month for life; the woman in lieu of her $100,000 lump sum benefit, is entitled to a retirement benefit of only $950 a month for life. The difference between the two annuity benefits is due to the woman's longer life expectancy. The insurance company that issues the annuity contract expects the average woman to live longer than the average man, and, therefore, if both the man and the woman are going to spend the same amount of money— $100,000—the woman must receive a lesser periodic benefit because she will collect it for a longer period of time.

Many plans in force today provide this choice, which, according to *Manhart*, appears to discriminate against women. After all, when the lesser $950 annuity is provided to the female, no one can ascertain that in fact this individual female will live longer than her male counterpart receiving the $1,000 benefit. Is not the employer then discriminating against the individual female employee? (Note that insurance companies, because they are not regulated by Title VII, are permitted to discriminate between males and females who purchase annuities. Only the employer is prohibited from discriminating, not insurance companies—except in their own role as employer.)

The answer may be that in order to assure equal benefits for men and women, the plan will have to provide that both the male and female in our example can receive either $100,000 in a lump sum or an annuity of $975 a month for life. In other words, instead of calculating annuities for males under one table and for females under another table, one table would be used for both. Such a table is commonly referred to as a unisex table because annuity benefits for all persons of similar age are equal, regardless of sex. Although this may seem like a viable solution, it does not, in fact, work. Every male would probably elect to receive a lump sum distribution of $100,000, go on his own to an insurance company, and purchase an annuity that pays $1,000 a month for life. Meanwhile, the female will elect to receive a $975-a-month annuity, which exceeds in value the $100,000 lump sum distribution. (Remember, it is assumed that a woman with

$100,000 at age 65 could purchase only a $950-a-month benefit if a unisex table is not used.) This situation is impossible because the unisex $975-a-month amount payable represents a decrease in the value of benefits a male would otherwise receive and an increase in the value of benefits a female would otherwise receive. In effect, the men are subsidizing the women. However, if the males are not required to take the $975 a month, no one would be funding the cost of providing this increased benefit to the females.

Is the solution, then, in profit-sharing plans, that participants will be unable to receive lump sum distributions and will be forced to collect annuities? In this manner, males will receive annuity benefits under a unisex table and subsidize the female annuity benefits. Currently, a number of cases are pending that deal with various Teachers Insurance and Annuity Association of American (TIAA-CREF) plans where individual accounts are maintained for participants with benefits paid based on sex-based annuity tables. Lump sum distributions from these plans are prohibited. Certain women are suing for the plans to use the unisex table.

Imagine the position of a company sponsoring a profit-sharing plan that has used sex-based annuity tables to calculate benefits. For years many women have elected annuity benefits in lieu of lump sum benefits and have received lesser monthly annuity payments than the men. On the basis of *Manhart*, all the female retirees sue for increased benefits, charging that the annuity policy constituted unlawful sex discrimination. Although the additional monthly benefits that *each* retired female might collect may be a relatively small sum, the *total* restitution bill owed to the millions of retired female employees could impose a staggering liability that would undermine the financial health of many employers. If the Supreme Court in the future grants retroactive relief, this fear could become a reality.

However, *Manhart* is not a strictly pro-female decision. Another example will demonstrate how men may wind up as the potential claimants in a lawsuit based on the implications of *Manhart*. Assume that a male and a female are participants in a company pension plan and that, on retirement at age 65, each is entitled to 50 percent of his or her average salary for life. Each had earned an average of $24,000 a year; on retirement, each is entitled to receive $1,000 a month for life. The plan provides that in lieu of the $1,000 periodic annuity payments, the retirees can receive the equivalent value in a lump sum—the man can receive $100,000 and the woman $110,000. The woman is receiving a greater lump sum benefit because she has a greater life expectancy than her male counterpart and requires greater funds in order to receive her $1,000 a month; when she surrenders the $1,000-a-month benefit, she is surrendering a more valuable asset than the male who is surrendering the same $1,000-a-month benefit. Can the man sue and claim that he, too, is entitled to $110,000? After all, Title VII and the Equal Pay Act require equal pay for equal work, regardless of sex. In other words, even as men cannot receive more pay than women for equivalent work, women cannot receive greater pay than men for equivalent work. Simply stated, the law prohibits favoring women over men, and therefore the man, in our example, sues to receive a $110,000 lump sum benefit.

Now the nightmare is complete. Every female in the profit-sharing plan is suing for damages, and every male in the pension plan is suing for damages. There is an obvious solution—one that would save employers from these staggering lawsuits. In the profit-sharing plan, where the female employees are getting lesser benefits, companies can lower the male benefits to equal those of the females. On the other hand, in the case of the pension plan, employers can declare that all females will receive not the greater benefit (of $110,000) but the lesser male benefit (of $100,000). This solution poses one serious drawback. The Equal Pay Act prohibits rectifying sex discrimination violations by lowering benefits paid to the persons discriminated against. The Supreme Court has not ruled whether this law is applicable to pension and profit-sharing plans; therefore, the feasibility of this solution is not yet known.

Many more dilemmas need to be examined. Reconsider the pension plan discussed previously. Under the plan, the man and woman, upon retiring, can each receive $1,000 a month for life. In order to avoid discriminating against males, the plan is amended to prohibit lump sum payments, and women can no longer receive greater lump sum amounts than do men. Everything seems sound, with the man and woman each receiving the same benefit of $1,000 a month for life. However, one man charges sex discrimination and sues the company that sponsors the pension plan. He argues: My life expectancy upon retirement is three years less than my female counterpart's. Therefore, you will be paying her $1,000 a month for three years more than you will be paying me. That adds up to $36,000. We both worked the same number of years for the company, for the same salary, and I think it unfair that the female would receive a greater pension benefit than I. He sues for $36,000. Should he collect? Undoubtedly, some male will sue on these grounds, and the courts will provide us with an answer to his question.

If you are not yet convinced that *Manhart* has thrown total confusion into the employee benefits area, consider one final situation. An employer has a life insurance program whereby all employees in the company are entitled to $20,000 of coverage. Upon the death of any employee, the designated beneficiary receives $20,000. However, the cost of providing this benefit is greater for male employees than for female employees because males have a shorter life expectancy, and their beneficiaries will collect life insurance sooner. Does this constitute a form of sex discrimination against females? After all, in order to provide the $20,000 benefit, the employer is spending more for each man than for each woman.

Conclusion

The numerous questions raised by *Manhart* beg for answers. These are vital questions and affect the retirement and life insurance benefits received by millions of Americans. The Supreme Court gave little indication about the answers. In this sense, *Manhart* resembled the decision in *Bakke*. Neither case gives any clear guidelines about reverse discrimination or sex discrimination effects on pension and other employee benefit plans. *Bakke* was limited to the strict facts before it, as was *Manhart*, following the judicial philosophy that calls for decisions only on cases directly before a court. The theory is that the plaintiff and defendant in a given case are concerned only with their particular situation, not with providing the court sufficient information to enable it to decide ancillary or similar cases that may arise in the future. In both *Bakke* and *Manhart*, the Supreme Court Justices seemed mesmerized by that rule of law which states that "hard cases make bad laws," and limited the scope of their decisions in these hard cases lest they make bad laws. However, by so circumscribing the scope of their decisions in *Bakke* and *Manhart*, the Court has declined to provide sorely needed guidance in two important areas of law.

One final fact is worthy of mention. As noted earlier, Title VII of the Civil Rights Act of 1964 prohibits employers from discriminating against any individual "with respect to his compensation terms, conditions, or privileges of employment, because of such individual's race, color, religion, sex, or national origin." One should hesitate before arguing that Congress intended, when it passed this law, to rectify all forms of sex discrimination. It was a Virginia congressman, opposed to the entire thrust of Title VII, particularly the provision for racial equality, who added the word "sex" to the Bill in an attempt to sabotage it. Matters did not turn out quite the way he thought.

Auditing Your Compensation Program for EEO Compliance

Stanley Kaufman

The concept of employment discrimination has evolved significantly since the passage of The Civil Rights Act of 1964 and President Johnson's signing of Executive Order 11246 in 1965. At that time, the thrust of the government was aimed at correcting specific, obvious discrimination such as segregated facilities, separate union locals for blacks and whites, refusal to hire minorities, and overt harassment of minorities and women. As these problems were remedied, however, the EEOC and compliance agencies focused their attention on relieving inequitable personnel practices, such as seniority practices and employment tests, which appeared fair but were actually a form of discrimination. Recently there has been emphasis on correcting compensation violations. Newspapers and legal journals increasingly report wage/salary increases and back-pay settlements awarded to discriminatees.

This article defines the obligations of federal contractors regarding discrimination in compensation, and suggests procedures for an internal compensation audit aimed at identifying and resolving problems which have a discriminatory effect.

The Letter of the Law

The first sentence in the EEO clause of every federal contract a company signs reads, "The contractor will not discriminate against

Mr. Kaufman is Contract Compliance Specialist, Office of Equal Opportunity, Energy Research and Development Administration, Washington, D.C.

any employee or applicant for employment because of race, color, religion, sex, or national origin." (Executive Order 11246.) Discrimination in "rates of pay or other forms of compensation" is included.

Administrative responsibility for the Executive Order is charged to the Secretary of Labor; other federal agencies are responsible for obtaining compliance by government contractors. The Secretary of Labor established the Office of Federal Contract Compliance Programs (OFCCP) to issue rules, regulations, and orders to insure implementation of the Executive Order by these compliance agencies. The OFCCP grouped American industry on the basis of Standard Industrial Classification (SIC) Codes and assigned each compliance agency companies by industries, regardless of which federal agencies the companies have contracts with.

Thus, when a compliance agency conducts a review, it is attempting to determine whether the company is fulfilling the EEO clause of its federal contracts. The compliance under OFCCP ultimately can authorize the cancellation of a corporation's government contracts.

Outlining the Audit

There is no simple solution to remedying discriminatory compensation practices. However, financial liability can be minimized through the preventive action of conducting an internal compensation audit designed to identify and do away with discriminatory compensation practices. Such an audit will correct these practices before they become more widespread, will pinpoint the need for rewriting compensation policy to forestall the occurrence of such problems in the first place, and will bring to light EEO problems in other personnel procedures.

The EEO compensation audit should be conducted facility by facility rather than on a company-wide basis. Corporate policies are implemented by many people, and no two people would interpret a given salary policy or guideline identically. Thus, to compare the compensation practices of a corporate headquarters in New York with a plant in West Virginia could be very misleading, despite applicability of the same policy manual at both locations.

The compensation audit should consist of three stages: first, preparing for the audit; second, conducting the audit; and third, reporting the audit.

The first step of audit preparation calls for studying background information to get a general feel for federal EEO requirements and how they affect the organization. Corporate EEO managers can help greatly in this regard, particularly in interpreting how laws and regulations are actually implemented.

Next, examine the findings and results of *recent* compliance reviews undertaken at some of the company's facilities and at facilities of other corporations. The word *recent* must be emphasized because the EEO area continually undergoes significant change.

After the background information is digested, gather the compensation data that is to be analyzed during the audit. Include all pertinent formal company policies, procedures, and guidelines. Key storehouses of these data are the compensation section of the company's policy manual, any updating policy memoranda and guidelines, and copies of the facility's current and past union agreements. Any informal compensation practices which have the effect of policy should also be included. This can be accomplished during a brainstorming session with company representatives from compensation, personnel, and supervision. This is vital because the thrust of the audit will be to compare policies (whether formal or informal) to practices, to determine if enforcement for minorities and women is the same as for nonminority men.

Next, gather the data to be used during the audit. A computer printout of employees used to prepare for an on-site compliance review should provide most of the necessary information. This listing should be broken down by organizational unit and include each employee's name; race; sex; date of hire; job hired into; date of assignment to and title of present job classification; EEO-1 category of present job classification; current rate of pay; date, amount, and type (e.g., merit increase, promotion, etc.) of last salary increase; educational level achieved; and merit rating.

Additional records referred to on a spot-check basis during the audit should include personnel files, management development, resumes, job descriptions, and overtime logs.

Once this background information has been assimilated and the data collected, the audit can proceed. Each aspect of compensation to be analyzed, whether it be hiring practices or allocation of overtime, should have as its audit goal identification of discrepancies between compensation policies and practices that result in lower wages, salaries, or benefits for minorities and women.

As a practical matter, investigative time can be shortened by asking three questions regarding the specific area of compensation under study:

(1) What is the normal occurrence?

(2) What variations occur frequently?

(3) What are the rare and unusual variations?

After answering these three questions for nonminority males, look at the data on minorities and women. If the answers for nonminority males differ from the answers for minorities and women, there is a problem requiring corrective action.

Audit Topics

The most basic analysis to make during the audit pertains to equal pay for equal work. Very simply, do minorities and women earn the same as nonminority men performing the same or similar work? The three major factors which must be considered here are:

(1) The date the employees were hired by the company;

(2) The length of time the employees have performed in the job; and

(3) Performance appraisal histories.

If two people have worked for the company a similar amount of time, have worked in the job a similar amount of time, and have a similar performance appraisal history, it is reasonable to expect the two to receive the same rate of pay.

Equal pay for equal work can also relate to temporary assignments. One plant, short of personnel to perform a relatively high-paying hourly job due to a flu epidemic, promoted six employees, including one black, from lower-paying jobs to fill in until the absentees returned to work. The five white employees received a wage differential for performing at the higher-rated job, but the black didn't. The company was obligated to pay the wage differential to the black employee.

Analyze whether wages and sarlaries paid to newly hired minorities and women discriminate. For example, are white male hires always placed within the ranges assigned to their positions, and minorities and women occasionally hired below minimum? If so, and if this were discovered by a compliance officer, wage and salary increases and back pay would be recommended.

Another analysis necessary to the audit is determining the basis on which merit increases are granted minorities and women. Are they bypassed for merit increases in violation of company policy and practice? Have any minorities or women received smaller merit increases than their nonminority or male counterparts given similar performance appraisals?

For example, according to the Compensation Policy Manual, a "B" performance rating may merit anywhere from a six percent to a nine percent salary increase. If a supervisor tends to award female "B" employees a six percent increase and male "B" employees a nine percent increase, he may be within company guidelines, but his practice discriminates against women.

Do minorities or women receive lower merit ratings and hence lower merit increases because of their race or sex? If so, then EEO sensitivity training for supervisors would be a necessary remedial action—along with the appropriate salary adjustments. Another area deserving analysis is promotions. Look at the average length of time between promotions. Assuming similar merit ratings, if minorities or women have had to wait longer, or if they have received smaller wage or salary promotional increases, then corrective action should be taken.

A facility's job evaluation plan should be examined for problems such as separate progression lines and wage rates for men and women; assignment of minorities or women to lower-paying job classifications than Caucasians or males performing comparable work; and the assignment of lower wage ranges to jobs occupied by women than jobs filled by men despite their having the same point value. A facility had divided its blue-collar work force into "heavy" jobs and "light" jobs. The heavy jobs were almost exclusively filled by men and the light jobs were predominantly filled by women. When evaluated by a factor comparison method and then assigned labor grades, the light jobs averaged three grades and twenty-eight cents per hour less than the "heavy" jobs despite having the same point value.

Upon discovery of this differential, the company immediately upgraded the light jobs by three labor grades, provided the women with up to two years' back pay based on the hourly difference, and encouraged them to move into the heavy jobs.

When studying nonexempt jobs, review overtime policies and practices to assure that minorities and women are provided an equal opportunity to work overtime.

A related problem is the assignment of duties and responsibilities to minorities or women clearly beyond those for which they are being paid. A common problem is that of a secretary with ten or fifteen years' experience in the personnel department. She knows the personnel function inside out, hires the hourly job workers, administers the payroll and fringe benefits, etc. The personnel manager, a male, either retires or is promoted to another assignment, and he is replaced by another male who might be a recent college graduate or have one or two years of personnel experience. She winds up training him, and *he* winds up climbing the corporate ladder. Two problems are evident here: First, she has been performing at the level of a professional but has been paid at the level of a clerical; second, she was not considered for the personnel manager position because of her sex.

The remedial actions necessary to correct these injustices would be up to two years' back pay (to compensate for the time she began performing the professional aspects of her job to the date the new personnel manager was hired), and a salary increase to at least the salary given the new personnel manager; up to two years' back pay of the difference between her salary and that of the new personnel manager; and a commitment to encourage her to fill the next professional vacancy that occurs for which she qualifies.

Bring It All Together

Upon completion of the investigative phase of the audit, informal meetings should be held with supervisory and management personnel to weed out erroneous findings. The substantiated results should then be prepared as a report to management. It should include both the findings and the recommended remedial actions, with completion timetables for eliminating the policies and practices deemed discriminatory.

The remedial action can take many forms, depending on the problem. If, for example, a company's compensation policy states that "new employees normally should be hired within the range for their jobs," and it is discovered that a disproportionate number of minorities are hired below minimum, several recommendations should be made: First, the policy should be changed so that it reads "new employees should never be hired below the minimum rates assigned to their jobs." This will help prevent a recurrence of the problem. Second, those minorities hired below minimum should receive salary increases of the amount of difference between their hire rates and at least the minimums for their jobs, and retroactive pay of the amounts of earnings lost had they not been hired below minimum. (Back pay should normally extend backward from the date the adverse action was corrected to either two years prior to the date the problem was identified or the date the adverse action occurred, whichever is more recent.) Third, the minorities' fringe benefits negatively affected by the adverse hire rate should be adjusted accordingly. If, for example, their retirement benefits depend on their total earnings while employed by the company, then their totals should be increased by the amount of their earnings lost as a result of the adverse hiring action.

The final step of the audit should be to identify and file all support data generated by the audit for possible use in a compliance review.

In conclusion, then, a vigorous internal EEO compensation audit followed up by meaningful corrective action—all undertaken on a voluntary basis—will go a long way toward removing the conditions that could lead to a painful, expensive, and embarrassing EEO compliance review, and should also minimize the number and magnitude of EEO complaints and lawsuits related to compensation filed against the company.

SELECTION

Cooperative Validation— Answer to the Validation Dilemma?

Stephen E. Bemis

All employers want to select qualified people for jobs but, in trying to do so, find themselves in a dilemma. Federal testing guidelines require validation of all selection procedures that adversely affect the employment opportunities of minority or female applicants.[1] Yet the management attitude generally is that validation is an unusually complex and highly expensive process. Executives typically believe that their selection procedures are job-related (valid). They therefore dismiss as an unjustified expense the cost of doing a validation study to meet government guidelines.

Following a quota system—hiring "by the numbers"—was long believed to be the only legally acceptable alternative to validation of selection procedures. But employers have found that hiring people to fill a quota without proper regard for individual qualifications has been even more expensive from the standpoint of company welfare, employee morale, productivity, and the goodwill of customers as well as of stockholders.

Employers can end up in court under provisions of Title VII of the

Stephen E. Bemis, in Washington, D.C., is director of validation services for Information Science Incorporated, a nationwide human resource company.

Civil Rights Act of 1964 (or even the Civil Rights Acts of 1866 and 1870), or face the loss of contracts under provisions of Executive Order 11246, for using selection procedures that adversely affect employment opportunities of minorities and have not been validated in accordance with federal guidelines. But quota hiring can also get the employer into court on a "reverse discrimination" charge. This is a dilemma faced by employers who are actively seeking to improve opportunities for minorities and women as well as by those who want to do no more than the law requires. Use of sound selection techniques and procedures with demonstrated validity may be slightly more laborious and time-consuming than quota hiring, and therefore moderately expensive. Yet, over the long run, it clearly carries fewer legal risks and produces a greater return on investment.

Stories abound on the high costs of a validation study. There is a lot of truth in many of these stories. Conducting a good criterion-related validity study requires the leadership of somebody who understands both the psychometric procedures that need to be followed and the legal aspects of validation and selection as reflected in the guidelines and court decisions. Getting the services of such people is costly, regardless of whether they are employees or outside consultants. In addition, employees who participate in the study and supervisors who help evaluate performance must take time away from the job. These problems can be handled if top management gives its support for the validation effort.

But there is a more serious stumbling block: an employer may not have a sufficient number of employees in many classifications to conduct a statistically meaningful study that will permit verification of validation results on relevant gender and minority groups. Such samples were difficult to get when 30 was considered to be an adequate sample size, but recent research (e.g., Schmidt, Hunter, and Urry 1976)[2] has shown that minimum sample sizes should probably be much greater. (While a recent unpublished paper by Donald Schwartz, chief psychologist of the Office of Federal Contract Compliance Programs, questions some of Schmidt's assumptions, it is clear that correlations based on samples of 30 can be misleading).

Single company, single location, criterion-related validation studies are starting to look like dinosaurs. Some alternatives, all variations on the validation theme, are beginning to emerge. One attractive alternative, cooperative or shared-cost validation, was suggested in a 1978 article in *Fortune* magazine.[3] In a shared-cost, criterion-related validation study, several companies and/or locations of a company combine resources, efforts, and samples to produce a much stronger validation study than any single company or location could accomplish. One such shared-cost validation study conducted in cooperation with a number of public utilities will be briefly described as an example of this procedure.

Flagship Study

Eight public utilities with total employment of over 40,000 persons pooled their resources to validate a battery of tests for the identification of applicants capable of performing key jobs in the companies. These jobs involve the application of mechanical principles and skills in the installation, maintenance, and repair of energy distribution and utilization systems; applicants are likely to progress to these key jobs, which are above entry level, within a reasonable period of time.

The study was managed by a consultant firm that assured comparability at all locations. Coordinators at each of the companies worked closely with the consultants on all phases of the project.

The job analyses involved a number of thrusts. First, job descriptions for key jobs at each of the eleven hiring locations of these companies were studied, and job activity statements were written to describe primary jobs at each of the companies. These activity statements were verified by on-site visits and by subject matter expert review. Subject matter experts in each of the companies also identified which of the job activity statements applied to each of the key jobs. In addition, several of these subject matter experts met as a panel and, under the guidance of the author, identified the worker requirements (knowledge, abilities, skills, and other characteristics) needed to perform the key jobs. Subject matter experts in each of the companies then rated the relevance of each of these worker requirements to each of the key jobs. All worker requirements were then tied to specific task statements. Workers had either to bring to the job the knowledge, skills, abilities, and other characteristics required, or they had to be trained.

Considerable attention was given to the development of a meaningful criterion for the study. First, training programs used at companies that planned to participate were reviewed, and based on the extensive job analysis, a determination was made that the key jobs required workers to have the basic technical knowledge to be effective performers. Based on this review, a series of "hands-on" training modules were developed to be used with programmed training mate-

121

rial. This training required individuals to read the programmed training materials at their own pace, perform problems that involve the application of electric or gas principles, and answer questions about what they had learned. The amount of time used for various parts of the training (i.e., time taken to read each of the sections of the programmed text, time to complete the practice problems) was recorded. Specially constructed tests were administered to determine the extent of knowledge of the principles of gas and basic electricity each individual possessed both before and after training, and quizzes were given after completion of each of the seven training modules. From these measures, twenty-six criteria of success in the modules were derived. A combination of statistical and rational procedures was used to select four of these measures as final criteria in the study.

The predictor tests being considered for use in selection were administered to 637 technically naive employees or applicants, who worked their way through as many of the seven modules as they could complete in a 2½-day period. Males (236) and females (391), minorities (187) and nonminorities (440), participated in this phase of the study. (In addition, at each hiring location, applicants were tested on the experimental predictor in order to create a data base that could be compared across companies and hiring locations and that could be compared with test results for the module participants.

Solid support was obtained in the statistical correlations (high .60s) computed from this data for the use of certain standardized tests to predict applicant success in learning (measured by quizzes) and applying the basic principles needed to perform the key jobs (measured by success in completing modules). A comprehensive master report and individual reports tailored to the environments of each of the participating companies were provided to the firms.

Reasons to Consider Cooperative Studies

These are some of the reasons cooperative studies are superior to single-company validation "dinosaurs":

1. A better, more comprehensive, more defensible study is possible when the resources from several locations are combined.

2. Although the total study will cost more than a study done in just one location, the cost per company or per location is reduced considerably. Thus, the "pooling" approach helps to conserve scarce resources.

3. Combining samples from several locations makes it feasible to do a criterion-related study in situations where such an approach to validation is the preferred mode from both legal and psychological points of view—but otherwise would not be feasible.

4. Cooperative studies frequently permit analysis of the validity and fairness of the resulting test with various subgroups (e.g., men and women, blacks, Spanish-surnamed Americans).

5. The involvement of a number of facilities with slightly different jobs or job combinations makes the study more difficult to do but is a distinct strength in the long run. Such variance initially helps assure the relevance of the resulting test batteries in a particular company even after some aspects of the job may change, because those aspects were most likely included in the data from another company.

6. The involvement of several geographically separated facilities in a cooperative validation study makes it easier later to extend the resulting validity standards to new locations. This assumes sufficient commonality to justify the combination initially. The ability to extend the standards is determined by comparison of job activities performed by workers at each site and/or the relative importance of various worker characteristics to job success at each location.

7. When a large number of companies is involved in a cooperative study, ambiguous government guidelines may be defined more sharply through a process of "consensual validation." The Nuclear Regulatory Commission, for example, has guidelines for the psychological screening of nuclear power plant personnel. The utility *industry's* interpretation and concerted implementation of these guidelines through a cooperative validation study would help the regulatory agency to implement its standards in a realistic and acceptable way.

The Uniform Guidelines on Employee Selection Procedures encourage cooperative validation studies as a cost-effective way for employers to meet the guidelines. Paragraph 8A reads:

> *Encouragement of cooperative studies.* The agencies issuing these guidelines encourage employers, labor organizations, and employment agencies to cooperate in research, development, search for lawful alternatives, and validity studies in order to achieve procedures which are consistent with these guidelines.

The four agencies issuing the Uniform Guidelines are developing a series of questions and answers to interpret the Guidelines. A draft version of this "Q&A" was published in the *Daily Labor Report* in

September 1978. The answer to question 45 shows that the issuing agencies are still urging employers to validate on a shared-cost basis.

Question: "Do the Guidelines permit users to engage in cooperative efforts to meet the Guidelines?"

Answer: "Yes. The Guidelines not only permit but encourage such efforts. Where users have participated in a cooperative study which meets the validation standards of these Guidelines and proper account has been taken of variables which might affect the applicability of the study to specific users, validity evidence specific to each user will not be required."

In addition to the support for cooperative validation contained in the wording of the Uniform Guidelines, several of the signatory agencies have encouraged cooperative validation in other ways, including funding such studies on public jobs. The U.S. Employment Service in the Department of Labor has been conducting cooperative validation studies in conjunction with state employment services for some time. In addition, they have funded cooperative validation studies on Interviewer and Local Office Manager positions. In a 1974 publication interpreting OFCCP's testing guidelines existing at that time, the Department of Labor recommended cooperative validation as a solution to the sample size problem.[4]

The U.S. Civil Service Commission (now the Office of Personnel Management) has funded cooperative validation on a "priority" occupation (Firefighter) identified by the Equal Employment Opportunity Coordinating Council; it has also provided grants to validation consortiums through funding from the Intergovernmental Personnel Act.

The Department of Justice, through the Law Enforcement Assistance Administration, has funded cooperative research on another of the priority occupations (Police Officer).

Key Questions about Cooperative Studies

If cooperative validation is desirable in such situations, why have so few such studies been conducted? The answer isn't clear, but some questions that have been raised are discussed below.

1. Won't cooperative validation with others in the same industry raise antitrust questions?

Answer: Lawyers usually raise this question. Drew S. Days, III, assistant attorney general for the Civil Rights Division of the Justice Department, says he does not believe that cooperative validation efforts raise antitrust problems. He also quotes a September 24, 1974, memorandum from the assistant attorney general for the Anti-Trust Division expressing the same opinion.

2. Will I have to restructure the jobs in my company to make them fit the mold of the other companies participating in the study?

Answer: No. The jobs at each participating company would need to be studied to make sure of sufficient comparability to justify inclusion in the same sample. The purpose of this job analysis is to reflect jobs as they now exist, not to try to change them. Most cooperative validation studies are sufficiently flexible to permit a number of differences in jobs between sites and companies.

3. Isn't it much more difficult to manage a cooperative validation study than a study done at a single location?

Answer: Yes, but with proper planning and experience, such studies can be effectively managed.

4. If we participate in a cooperative validation study, and one of the other participating employers loses a court case over the use of the resulting selection procedures, won't the rest of the cooperating employers fall like dominoes?

Answer: Your exposure would be the same as it is any time you use standardized tests also used by other employers. (Consider the negative publicity for the Wonderlic and the Bennett tests after the *Griggs* decision.) If your use of a test is challenged because of the publicity associated with another employer's loss in court, you need validity data to support your use of that selection procedure. Cooperative validation is a way to get that data.

Any legal challenge to the use of a selection procedure will relate to its use in a specified set of circumstances. If the selection procedures are improperly used or if there are other problems in the recruitment or selection of minorities, the employer may lose. Other employers who are doing things properly should be able to defend their practices and procedures. This has been the experience with the

Police Officer battery developed by the Selection Consulting Center in California.

Conclusions

Cooperative validation is frequently the most cost-effective and legally defensible way of accomplishing what must be done to assure the job-relatedness and usefulness of selection procedures.

There are several ways to go about organizing a cooperative study. One is to work through a trade or business association. Another is for employers who have similar jobs (either in the same industry or different industries) to band together on their own. A third possibility is to get a consultant with experience in cooperative validation to put together a consortium for such a study. Whatever approach is taken, it should be done now. A cooperative study could be the answer to the validation dilemma.

NOTES

1. Department of Justice, Civil Service Commission, Equal Employment Opportunity Commission, and Department of Labor, "Uniform Guidelines on Employee Selection Procedures," 43, *Fed. Reg.* 166 (August 25, 1978).

2. F.L. Schmidt, J. E. Hunter, and V. W. Urry, "Statistical Power in Criterion-Related Validity Studies," *Journal of Applied Psychology,* 1976.

3. Lee Smith, "Equal Opportunity Rules Are Getting Tougher," *Fortune*, June 1978, pp. 152-156.

4. U.S. Department of Labor, *Questions and Answers on the OFCCP Testing and Selection Order*, 1974.

True Entrance Qualifications
and Objective
Performance Measures

Richard G. Vail and Richard F. Landrigan

Students of the snail's-pace development of EEO enforcement since the first "compliance reviews" of the President's Committee on Equal Employment Opportunity in 1961 perceive a dramatic shift in emphasis. In those early days, required posters, minority receptionists, and sizable contributions to the local Urban League evidenced an enlightened equal opportunity employer. No more!

The perspective back to the 1960s clearly points up the increasing sophistication of the EEO enforcement process. In the 1960's, prime emphasis was on integrating the workplace; now we are critically concerned with discrimination issues involving post-hire personnel decision-making. Overt failure-to-hire cases have become rare, replaced by sophisticated post-hire issues such as placement, promotion, performance appraisal, job content evaluation, job posting, and career pathing. Typical plaintiffs who formerly pursued individual charges, most often on the basis of race, have now become class action representatives, commonly seeking redress for systemic race and sex discrimination. From cases primarily concerned with hourly employees, we find more and more litigation revolving around "heavier" supervisory and managerial jobs. The EEO enforcement agencies have

Mr. Vail is Director of Employee Relations Services, Hay Associates, Philadelphia, PA.

Mr. Landrigan is Special Consultant-Employee Relations Services, Hay Associates, Boston, MA.

begun to understand and utilize the employer's computer capability in piecing together patterns of systemic discrimination. There appears to be every reason to believe that the process of sophistication will continue at its present rate, if not more rapidly. Awareness begets awareness and settlements beget settlements, as we have seen in the hundreds of progeny of the 1973 AT&T Consent Decree. The Carter Administration undoubtedly will provide more moral and financial support to EEO enforcement than prior administrations did.

But some things in this fast-moving area remain the same. The current theory of employment discrimination is still set forth in the Supreme Court's 1971 decision in *Griggs v. Duke Power Co.*:[1] any aspect of an employment system that "operates to exclude" persons protected under Title VII of the Civil Rights Act of 1964 is illegal unless it can be shown to be "job related" and a "business necessity." The employer almost universally loses the "business necessity" argument unless he can show significant aspects of public and/or employee safety,[2] or that his employment system did not "operate to exclude" or "adversely impact" upon protected persons.

Adverse Impact

Proof of adverse impact begins with a showing of statistical disparity of representation of one or more protected groups in an employer's work force as against the availability of such groups. Given the statistical disparity, EEO agencies and the courts examine the policies and procedures and their actual effect to determine what may have contributed to the imbalance. Increasingly, plaintiffs and enforcers are applying the statistical analysis required by Griggs to more detailed and complex aspects of the employment system and are asking more astute questions about policies, procedures, or corporate political realities that foster an employment system which "operates to exclude" persons protected under EEO laws.

American industrial society consistently has applied entrance qualification standards that exceed those actually required to perform a particular job at a competent level of performance. For example, degreed applicants have historically been preferred over the nondegreed without any analysis of whether the degree relates to ability to perform the job. The imposition of inflated standards for hire or promotion clearly "operate to exclude" the females and/or minorities who are protected under Title VII, even though those standards have been used primarily by white male managers to discriminate against other white male managers for reasons of corporate politics. The "good, better, best" system of selection and promotion without determination of what is truly required to perform a job is illegal under *Griggs* in practically all instances because:

- It creates "adverse impact" on protected persons, by "operating to exclude" them from jobs for which they are qualified;
- It is not "job related" to the extent that it requires qualifications that are not truly required for the job;
- It is not a "business necessity," since the employer has not analyzed and documented what is required to perform the job. Nor has the employer searched for alternative selection procedures that could accomplish the same objective with less adverse impact.[3]

The Office of Federal Contract Compliance Programs (OFCCP) recently investigated a complaint from a black female who had been denied a promotion to plant manager's secretary because she knew no shorthand. Prior incumbents testified that shorthand was not needed to perform the duties of the job. The agency concluded (correctly) that the employer did not know what tasks were actually performed in many of its jobs, did not know what entrance qualifications should properly be required for certain jobs, and did not know how to measure performance. The shorthand requirement operated to exclude minorities from promotional opportunities, and it was clearly not a business necessity since it was not a skill required to perform the job. The company was ordered to examine its entrance requirements for all jobs in two facilities in order to separate those that were needed from those that were not. The compliance agency made identification of these standards the price for stopping proceedings that would bar this employer from governmental contracts.

When the fact of historical inflation of entrance qualifications is combined with the reality that no employee is fully competent on his/her first day of work, a concept emerges that we believe will be critical to the future development of equal employment opportunity and human resources management.

Knowledges, Skills, and Abilities

Knowledges, skills, and abilities (KSA's) are required to perform jobs.[4] On the first day of work, a person who possesses the minimum qualification for a job is not fully "qualified" or "competent" because he/she has not acquired knowledges, skills, and abilities that are learned *on* the job (e.g., petty cash procedures, location of tool crib, etc.). In other words, one who possesses the minimum entrance qualifications is "qualifiable" and becomes "qualified" or "competent" over a period of time.

Experience with job analysis and EEO teaches two lessons:

- The true minimum qualifications for a job are often lower than supposed;
- Many elements of most jobs are learned after hire—on the job.

The process of establishing minimum qualifications for jobs can be succinctly described as "depuffing." The courts have been depuffing jobs since *Griggs*, when the Supreme Court decided that a high-school diploma requirement for certain jobs created adverse impact on blacks in a situation in which the employer could not prove business necessity. Since then, the courts have struck down numbers of formal education requirements that failed to survive the *Griggs* adverse-impact analysis. In each decision, the court—not the employer—established new minimum qualifications for the job. And the courts have not stopped at examining educational requirements; other entrance requirements held to create adverse impact include "time in grade" and "experience" in specific situations.

The EEO and other EEO enforcers are beginning to utilize the minimum-qualifications concept. The following language is included in the Commission's proposed "Guidelines on Remedial/Affirmative Action" as an indication of employer Title VII liability: the question is whether "percentages . . . are substantially similar to the percentages of those groups available in the workforce in the relevant job market who possess the *basic* job-related *qualifications*" (emphasis supplied). The government's perception of minimum qualifications is bound to become more clearly focused as enforcement personnel become better educated in such matters as job evaluation systems (used to determine job content and to compare jobs for pay purposes), which are now being viewed by the enforcers as a way to discover discrimination (in addition to their role as a tool for EEO compliance).

The process of determining minimum qualifications is almost always undertaken by employers for compliance reasons. Once completed, the process has myriad uses, even apart from EEO compliance: recruitment, promotion, placement, job posting, employee development, performance appraisal, job evaluation and compensation.

The Costs of Overqualification

Determining true entrance qualifications is clearly cost-effective, although this fact is often overlooked because of preoccupation with EEO ramifications. Employers have not yet recognized the financial benefits that accrue when it is no longer necessary to pay for education, experience, or skills not actually required to do a particular job. For employers who have identified minimum entrance qualifications, the days of paying an M.B.A. to perform work which could be done by the equivalent of a high-school diploma holder are over.

Selection of overqualified employees also can lead to job dissatisfaction. Its costs are reflected in absenteeism, accidents, high turnover, sloppy work, and work stoppages. Lesser- but at least minimally qualified job candidates might well find interesting and challenging what the overqualified worker finds repetitive and deadening.

Perhaps the ultimate act of EEO compliance on the part of an employer is the restructuring of jobs to accommodate protected persons. Mental and physical handicap are most often mentioned in this context, but accommodation can (and will) also relate to age, sex, national origin, or even race. The information readily available when job tasks and minimum entrance qualifications have been identified enables the enlightened employer to regroup and rearrange the various pieces of jobs in order to create new jobs that can be performed by protected persons. By the same token, the new, relatively simple jobs created also result in other enriched jobs as more complex tasks are joined together for the first time.

Minimum qualifications bear an essential relationship to an area that will be of critical importance in the brave new world of EEO: objective performance measures and the standards derived from those measures. Just as entrance job requirements have historically operated to exclude females and minorities from the better jobs, so have most performance appraisal systems traditionally operated in much the same manner. Performance appraisal is a subtle—but perhaps the ultimate—employer "test": it not only affects, but usually controls, pay increases, promotion, placement, career path, layoff, and, most importantly, the perceptions of the employee held by the organization's decision makers. Obviously, performance standards are based upon someone's scale of values as to what barely acceptable, competent, or superior performance is all about. Unfortunately, that scale of values often belongs to a white male who participates in some sort of "old boy network" and—perhaps unconsciously—applies that network's values. The many performance evaluation systems that "operate to exclude" protected persons will continue to run into problems with *Griggs* since they flunk the business necessity test.

Subjective tests are almost universal. Female and minority employees are usually judged by white male members of "the club" according to inbred values, including the ability to relate to the other members by sharing their values. Measuring an employee and his/her future on the basis of "adaptability, bearing, demeanor, manner, verbal expression, appearance, maturity, drive, and social behavior"[5] operates to exclude those who are different from the appraiser.

The combination of subjective measures and statistics proving adverse impact has consistently resulted in hostile receptions in court. This has been true whether the subjective process has been used for promotion, hiring, training, layoff, or performance appraisals affecting the employee's future. The Supreme Court has also decided that subjective supervisory judgments are not to be used as a measure of a test's ability to predict success on a particular job.[6] A recent case applied *Griggs* principles to strike down a performance appraisal system that adversely impacted on older workers; perhaps this is a precursor of things to come.[7]

On most employers' payrolls are large "affected classes"[8] of protected persons; this could result in back-pay awards or settlements of a size sufficient to have a major impact on the operations of the organization if class charges are filed. The statistical probability of an employer escaping a confrontation with its Title VII "affected class" liability becomes less with each passing year. The only way an employer can minimize this liability is to reduce it, starting by promoting and transferring minorities and females into all areas of the organization. Only the process of removing the artifical barriers to jobs and changing the demographics of the work force will reduce liability. Truly job-related entrance requirements and job-related objective performance measures are the tools management needs to open up jobs to those previously shut out.

It is clear that both entrance job qualifications and performance measures are "tests" under the rationale of *Griggs* and EEOC and OFCCP regulations. Although the relative merits of the "validation" issue are beyond the scope of this article, it is emphasized that numerous courts and agencies have stressed the necessity for a professional "job analysis" to provide the foundation for a "valid" test. The latest "Proposed Uniform Guidelines on Employee Selection Procedures," issued in December 1977 by the Civil Service Commission, EEOC, Department of Justice, and Department of Labor, stress the need for job analysis, stating that "enforcement agencies will take into account the fact that a thorough job analysis was conducted and that careful development and use of a selection procedure in accordance with professional standards enhance the probability that the selection procedure is valid for the job."

The obligation of employers to carefully examine their job qualification requirements and eliminate those that "operate to exclude" and are not a "business necessity" has been specifically required since the issuance of the 1970 EEOC Guidelines and was reaffirmed by the Supreme Court in *Griggs*. The job analysis process, if successfully carried through, will result in the establishment of minimum qualifications; these will either (1) eliminate or demonstrate the absence of adverse impact and thereby eliminate a *Griggs* problem, or (2) articulate a "business necessity" defense where there is no way to eliminate the "adverse impact" against protected persons in terms of minimum entrance job requirements. The job analysis process also forms an excellent basis for the precise determination of objective performance appraisal criteria that accurately measure only those tasks that are actually performed.

The court decisions and the various regulations do not specify how the job analysis process should be undertaken or what elements should be included. Without the benefit of more specific guidance, alternative methods are clearly acceptable as long as they result in an elimination of "adverse impact" and, where they do not, provide "business necessity" documentation.

Our own approach commences with an initial "task analysis" to identify the actual tasks performed on the job. This is accomplished by detailed interviews with incumbents, supervisors, line and staff personnel, and management. The critical KSA's needed to perform the various tasks in a competent manner are determined. If those participating in the task analysis disagree as to whether a task is performed or not, the incumbent, supervisors, and others with knowledge of the job are consulted immediately for resolution of the issue. The information-gathering process must be totally accurate, or the minimum qualifications identified will be useless. The end result is a document differing from a standard job description: It not only describes fully acceptable, competent performance, but also identifies the minimum qualifications needed for minimally acceptable performance *at hire* without benefit of any on-the-job training. The document also reflects pooled judgments of all those involved in the process, a technique which is looked upon favorably by the government.

The process outlined has been applied to jobs at all levels of a work force in various industrial settings. The more complex the job, however, the more time consuming the basic incumbent interview becomes, as well as the review process in general. Whereas the task analysis is relatively straightforward in the case of most nonexempt jobs, it is more accurate to lump tasks into areas of end-result accountabilities when dealing with the minimum qualifications for managerial or executive jobs. On the other hand, it is quite simple to keep the process up to date in the event that duties change in any job, due to the format of the documentation.

"Least Qualified Incumbent" Standard

Minimum qualifications that have not been "depuffed" are well-nigh worthless. A critical cross-check is the "least qualified incumbent" standard. This compares the entrance qualifications of the minority or female who is "excluded" with those that the "least qualified incumbent" (usually a white male) possessed at the time that person was hired. If the "least qualified incumbent" is being paid every Friday, it is useless to argue to EEO enforcers that he/she is not meeting at least the minimum acceptable standards of the job. The "least qualified incumbent" standard has been applied by several courts and is appearing more frequently in recent consent decree settlements between employers and the EEOC. The 1977 proposed "Uniform Guidelines on Employee Selection Procedures" warn against applying even a "validated" selection procedure to employees or applicants who were denied equal treatment without extending the same opportunities that existed for other employees or applicants in the past unless the employer can show than any increase in selection standards is required by business necessity. It is especially important to apply the "least qualified incumbent" standard where incumbents do not possess the same educational degrees or specialized experience that management now requires of new hires.[9]

From the task analysis and minimum qualifications determinations, accurate and timely objective performance measures can be developed. These measures directly relate to the minimum qualifications in the sense that they are based upon the critical tasks or end-result accountabilities identified earlier. Performance measures (e.g., units produced per worker-hour by shift for a production supervisor) then become the basis of performance standards (5,000 units per shift

= *standard*; 10,000 units per shift = *outstanding*). These standards are then applied to all employees in the same job classification (perhaps after job incumbents and their supervisors have agreed upon target goals for the performance rating period).

The minimum qualifications/performance measures process is an idea whose time has come, and it will become and remain one of the most important management tools ,in the human resources area long after most employers feel that problems of massive EEO liability have been adequately handled.

It should be understood that the identification and implementation of minimum entrance qualifications expressed as demonstrable KSA's do not necessarily lower existing standards for job entrance. Nor do they prevent employers from raising minimum standards for business necessity reasons or in circumstances where no EEO problem exists. Furthermore, the implementation of this process does not necessarily prevent employers from changing jobs, altering periods of time within which employees must become qualified, or shifting emphasis from one performance measure to another. In each case, however, identification of minimum entrance qualifications and performance measures provides the information base for intelligent decision making. Similarly, in the hiring situation, knowledge of minimum entrance qualifications permits precise definition of who should be in the applicant pool for a particular job, based on the KSA's they currently possess. Moreover, this knowledge assists the employer in the individual selection decision by delineating excess entrance qualifications and allowing them to be matched with the knowledge, skills, and abilities to be acquired on the job. Even though total or perfect utilization of an employer's human resources is unattainable, we view the identification of minimum entrance qualifications and objective performance measures as the most effective management effort toward that goal.

NOTES

1. *Griggs v. Duke Power Co.*, 401 U.S. 424 (1971).

2. *Spurlock v. United Airlines*, 475 F.2d 216 (10th Cir. 1972); *Carey v. Greyhound Bus Co.*, 500 F.2d 1372 (5th Cir. 1974); *Hodgson v. Tamiami Trail Tours, Inc.*, 531 F.2d 224 (5th Cir. 1976).

3. See Uniform Guidelines on Employee Selection Procedures (EEOC) 29 CFR Part 1607, 12/30/77, Section 3(B). These *proposed* guidelines have been issued by EEOC, Department of Justice, Department of Labor and the Civil

Service Commission, and will hereinafter be referred to as the Consensus Guidelines to reduce confusion with earlier drafts.

4. A number of EEO regulations specifically refer to "knowledges, skills, and abilities" as items to be examined in conjunction with job analysis, including Proposed Consensus Guidelines Sec. 14(c) 1, 15(c) 3.

5. *Robinson v. Union Carbide*, 538 F.2d 652 (5th Cir. 1976).

6. *Moody v. Albemarle Paper Co.*, 422 U.S. 496 (1975).

7. *Mistretta v. Sandia Corp.*, 15 EPD ¶ 7902 (DC NM 1977).

8. OFCCP defines an affected class as "those who continue to suffer the consequences of discrimination." 41 C.F.R. Part 60.2.1(b).

9. Vernon Jordan, Executive Director of the Urban League, told the League's 1975 convention that EEO would force American industry to tolerate the same degree of incompetence from blacks that historically it has tolerated from whites.

Employee Selection Procedures—Uniform Guidelines at Last

Susan A. Cahoon

The Uniform Guidelines on Employee Selection Procedures took effect September 25, 1978, in substantially the same form in which they were originally proposed.

In recent years most employers have found themselves subject to different, and at times conflicting, sets of guidelines on employee selection procedures: the EEOC's 1970 "Guidelines on Employee Selection Procedures," 29 C.F.R. § 1607, and the OFCCP's 1971 "Testing and Selecting Employees by Government Contractors," 41 C.F.R. § 60-3. An important development in equal opportunity law has been the publication of a new set of selection guidelines released by EEOC, the Departments of Justice and Labor, and the Civil Service Commission under the title "Proposed Uniform Guidelines on Employee Selection Procedures." 42 Fed. Reg. 65542 (Dec. 30, 1977). To appreciate fully the significance of the proposed guidelines, which will be referred to in the remainder of this article as the "Uniform Guidelines," it is necessary to review the events that culminated in their release, to summarize their important features, and then to comment upon potential problems in achieving a truly uniform approach by the federal enforcement agencies.

Miss Cahoon, J.D. cum laude, Harvard University, is a partner in the Atlanta, Georgia, and Washington, D.C., firm of Kilpatrick, Cody, Rogers, McClatchey & Regenstein. She frequently represents employers in employment discrimination litigation.

Origins of the "Guidelines" Concept

Within a year after the effective date of Title VII of the Civil Rights Act of 1964, EEOC, as the agency charged with responsibility for administering the new statute, released a short document entitled "Guidelines on Employment Testing." This was little more than an exhortation to employers to adopt a "total assessment'" philosophy rather than to screen out minority or female candidates on the basis of a single factor such as a diploma or degree requirement, test score, etc. Although EEOC had power to offer employers technical guidance on compliance, it lacked staff or inclination to provide either more specific guidelines or individualized commentary on an employer's selection practices.

As testing practices became a major focus of Title VII litigation, EEOC followed the lead of the OFCC (predecessor to the present OFCCP), which had published a much more comprehensive set of guidelines in 1968 addressed specifically to validation,[1] and released its own detailed "guidelines" in 1970.

In contrast to its earlier, generalized guidelines, EEOC's 1970 guidelines reviewed alternative strategies for validating employment selection procedures. Among other things, the guidelines arguably expressed a preference for criteria-related validation;[2] placed the burden on the employer to demonstrate that there was no alternative procedure with less adverse impact on minorities or females than the one he was using; and stressed the need to explore whether "differential validity"[3] might exist. EEOC's guidelines also seemed to require that every step of the selection process be validated, without regard to whether the total results produced any adverse impact on a protected group. The 1970 EEOC guidelines, like OFCC's 1968 guidelines, sought to impress upon employers the need to analyze their selection procedures by techniques that industrial psychologists found acceptable in their own work.[4]

Because most litigation against employers has proceeded under Title VII—and, when race discrimination is at issue, under the parallel anti-discrimination provisions of the Civil Rights Act of 1871, 42 U.S.C. § 1981—most judicial opinions that have discussed testing guidelines have concentrated upon EEOC's guidelines for complying with Title VII. Although neither the 1966 nor 1970 guidelines were adopted under the more stringent rule-making procedures for federal administrative agencies, the Supreme Court has held that, at least to the extent the guidelines seek to require employers to utilize job-related procedures, they are consistent with the intent of Congress and therefore entitled to "great deference." See, e.g., *Griggs v. Duke Power Co.*, 401 U.S. 424 (1971); *Albemarle Paper Co. v. Moody*, 422 U.S. 405 (1975). However, specific provisions of the guidelines have met with varying fates. For example, the ostensible preference in the 1970 EEOC guidelines for criteria-related validation has been sometimes followed and other times rejected.[5] The admonition to try differential validity studies was endorsed in the same opinion that ruled that the plaintiff in a discrimination suit has the burden of offering evidence that there exist suitable, less adverse alternatives to the employer's job-related practices. *Albemarle Paper, supra.*

The competing OFCC guidelines were less important as litigation tools, but they were of obvious practical concern to anyone doing business with the federal government. One of the significant differences between the 1970 EEOC guidelines and the government contractor guidelines was that the latter, and related interpretive materials, made it clear that criteria-related, content, and construct validation methods are equally acceptable. OFCC also released supplementary bulletins announcing its position that the duty to validate a selection procedure would not be triggered unless the overall selection process resulted in a selection ratio for the minority or female segment of the relevant population that was less than 80 percent of the selection ratio for the majority or male population. Those charged with enforcing Executive Order 11246 adopted a "bottom line" approach (i.e., examination of results of the employer's selection practices as a whole) and established the "80 percent rule" for determining when the duty to validate is triggered.

In addition to the government contract compliance machinery and EEOC, other federal agencies, such as the Department of Justice, have also had some responsibility for interpreting and enforcing employment discrimination laws. The Civil Service Commission developed internal guidelines on validation and served as the compliance agency responsible for processing most discrimination complaints by federal employees.

When Title VII was amended by the Equal Employment Opportunity Act of 1972, a new coordinating body—the Equal Employment Opportunity Coordinating Council (EEOCC)—was established. EEOCC was designed to harmonize the fragmented approaches to enforcement of the overlapping requirements of Title VII, Executive Order 11246, federal civil service regulations, etc. One of EEOCC's first projects was to try to develop a set of uniform guidelines on employee selection procedures that would be used by all federal agencies responsible for fairness in employee selection.

However, by November 1976, despite four years of effort, no agreement had been reached on a uniform set of guidelines. Finally, the Departments of Labor and Justice and the Civil Service Commission, which had agreed among themselves on the content of an appropriate set of guidelines, proceeded to issue their own selection guidelines, "Federal Executive Agency Guidelines on Employee Selection Procedures." In the same month EEOC republished its 1970 guidelines.

After months of additional discussion and debate, the four agencies agreed at last upon a new set of guidelines. The public was given until March 7, 1978 to submit written comments, and a public hearing on the proposed guidelines was held on April 10.

As of this writing, the uniform guidelines have not yet been officially adopted. Many comments have been submitted, and there has been vigorous debate. The remaining sections of this article will discuss the proposed guidelines and some of their more troublesome features. The criticisms are typical of those submitted in the written comments from concerned members of the public or in the testimony at the public hearing.

Basic Features of the
Proposed Uniform Guidelines

The proposed guidelines were designed to supersede all previous guidelines on employee selection procedures. They purport to have been "built upon court decisions, the previously issued guidelines. . . , and the practical experience of the agencies, as well as the standards of the psychological profession." Major features include:

• *A broad definition of what is covered.* The proposed Uniform Guidelines clearly apply not only to tests in the traditional sense but also to any other selection procedures used as a basis for "any employment decision."

• *Requirement of use of the less adverse procedure "where two or more selection procedures are available which are substantially equally valid for a given purpose."* The Uniform Guidelines adopt somewhat of a compromise between the apparent judicial standard for burden of proof (by showing that a selection procedure with adverse impact is job related an employer shifts to plaintiff the burden of showing that suitable less restrictive alternatives exist) and the preferred litigation position of plaintiffs (and some of the agencies), which would place upon the employer at the outset the duty to conduct a stringent "global" search for acceptable alternatives having less adverse impact. Instead, under the proposed guidelines the employer must make "a reasonable effort to become aware of such alternative procedures." It is impossible to predict what may be necessary to accomplish this objective. However, it would seem to require at a minimum that the test user survey current comparable tests and also make certain that his procedure is not more difficult than the actual work on the job.[6]

• *Detailed record-keeping requirements on adverse impact.* An employer must maintain extensive data by racial, ethnic or sex groups for both applicants and incumbent employees; no time limit has been set for retention of the data. Failure to keep these records authorizes a compliance agency to infer that adverse impact exists.

• *Definition of "adverse impact" based upon applying a combination of the bottom line concept and the 80 percent rule to the selection rate of the group in question in comparison to the most successful group.* The uniform guidelines do not require validation where there is no adverse impact. In view of this limited scope for the validation requirement, there are detailed instructions on the methodology the employer should use in determining when his duty to validate has been triggered.

The bottom line approach is expressly adopted so that if a selection process produces no adverse impact, then the individual components of the process need not be validated. (However, the enforcement agencies do not make an ironclad commitment that under no circumstances will they take enforcement action based upon a component's adverse impact.) The guidelines do require the individual evaluation of components of a selection process whenever the total selection process produces an adverse impact.

The 80 percent rule is adopted to determine when the adverse impact is significant enough to warrant enforcement action or surveillance. This statement is somewhat hedged by the inclusion of the following language: "Smaller differences in selection rates may nevertheless constitute adverse impact, where they are significant in both statistical and practical terms or where a user's actions have discouraged applicants disproportionately on racial, sex, or ethnic grounds." Conversely, the new guidelines do recognize that selection ratios that do not meet the 80 percent test may nevertheless not constitute adverse impact when they are the product of small numbers and lack statistical significance, or where special recruiting activities may have caused the pool of minority or female candidates to be atypical.

● *Recurring emphasis on affirmative action.* To an extent not found in prior guidelines, especially EEOC's, the new guidelines repeatedly emphasize an employer's affirmative action role. The references to affirmative action are consistent with EEOC's emphasis on bottom line results. However, they recognize that "selection procedures under such programs should be based upon the ability or *relative ability* to do the work as shown by properly validated selection procedures." [§ 4E, emphasis added.]

● *Acceptance of any professionally acceptable validation strategy and detailed standards of "minimum" validation requirements, with particular stringency for content and construct validation efforts.* The uniform guidelines reflect the professional position that content or construct validation is of equal dignity with criteria-related validation. In describing validation standards, strong emphasis is placed on the importance of a careful job analysis.

● *Somewhat less emphasis on the once-fashionable hypothesis of differential validity.* Whereas prior guidelines indicated briefly that an employer was required to investigate the possibility of differential validity whenever it was technically feasible to do so, the new guidelines list a number of circumstances that would render such studies technically infeasible.

● *Exclusion of guidance under the Age Discrimination Act of 1975 and under § 504 of the Rehabilitation Act of 1973.* Exclusion of these statutes from the guidelines may be affected by the President's reorganization plan, which will transfer to EEOC enforcement of the Equal Pay, Age Discrimination, and Rehabilitation acts.

● *Exclusion of coverage in determining the lawfulness of a seniority system.* The uniform guidelines apply only to selection procedures. They do not attempt to provide guidance about lawfulness of a seniority system, except to the extent that within the seniority system various selection procedures other than seniority are used to determine qualifications or ability to perform the job.

What of the Future?

If the uniform guidelines are adopted in their present form, one immediate and beneficial effect will be to lessen the employer's dilemma in attempting to comply with sometimes conflicting interpretations of federal laws regarding employment discrimination. By applying essentially a bottom line approach to defining adverse impact and by using the 80 percent rule as a measure of substantiality of adverse impact, the guidelines also make it easier for an employer to make an informed judgment about whether to embark upon a validation program. Similarly, they eliminate the confusion concerning whether there is a "preferred" validation method.

However, the guidelines are certain to generate their own confusion, and there are many provisions whose future course of interpretation is difficult to anticipate. For example, the attempted compromise on the employer's duty to investigate the availability of alternative selection procedures with less adverse impact is ambiguous. The guidelines do not define what constitutes "a reasonable effort" to learn of alternative procedures. The guidelines could, but do not, illustrate this provision with some examples of the sources of information to which a "reasonable" employer should refer. Moreover, defining alternative procedures, the phrase "substantial evidence of validity for the same job in similar circumstances" is quite vague. Presumably what is meant is a validity study meeting guideline requirements, or at least appearing to do so. If that is the intent, the provision should be made clearer. If it is not the authors' intent, then that fact should be indicated and some guidance provided to an employer concerning what the requisite lesser quantum of evidence may be.

Also, the guidelines rely upon too mechanistic an approach to the relevant comparison in utilizing the 80 percent rule. They speak in terms of "selection rate." However, that measure may be of little practical concern in situations where there are large numbers of candidates and only a small percentage of either group is successful. For example, if only 1 percent of the most successful group's applicants are hired and 0.79 percent of the protected group's applicants are hired, there is "adverse impact" under this definition. However, a comparison of rejection rates would be a more realistic approach to this situation. Another potential problem with the definition of the 80 percent rule is its effort to tie the comparison to the "rate for the group [racial, ethnic or sex] with the highest rate." It would be preferable to choose for comparison a group that is a major factor in the relevant labor market.

The requirements for criterion-related validation may generate substantial debate and confusion with respect to evaluating test fairness. This is perhaps understandable, for the profession of industrial psychology has difficulty in agreeing upon an appropriate definition of the concept—to say nothing of the proper technique for exploring whether an otherwise job-related test is "fair." The guidelines' somewhat gingerly treatment of the entire subject of what—if any—construct validation methodology is appropriate accurately reflects industrial psychology's generally confused state with respect to this technique.

It is sometimes argued that if, in the past, an employer had an easily met requirement for a job but excluded racial minorities from consideration for it, he cannot now open that job to minorities and simultaneously require that all candidates meet selection standards that are more difficult than the former ones. Although the courts have tended to permit the use of new job-related standards, the "disparate treatment" section of the Uniform Guidelines mandates that when these discriminatees seek to qualify an employer must use the old selection standards unless he can prove business necessity for the stricter standards. The Uniform Guidelines also indicate that an employer who had used invalid or unvalidated procedures in the past is not precluded from developing and using new procedures that comply with the guidelines. Read together, these provisions may produce the result that an employer who had no job-related standards during a period of active discrimination against a class may more readily adopt new, validated procedures and require that all employees meet them than can the employer who had used job-related standards but had barred minorities from consideration. This seems to be an anomalous result.

In the final analysis, whether the effort to achieve uniform guidelines will succeed depends upon the interpretations by the four agencies involved. At this moment, there is reason for genuine concern that the agencies do not agree upon a method for applying the guidelines. The EEOC apparently fears that employers might demonstrate that tests with adverse impact upon minorities or females are job-related; because of this fear, EEOC Chair Norton apparently hopes that EEOC will encourage employers not to use tests but instead, in order to escape the expenses of validation, to maintain a "bottom line" that has no adverse impact.

The ambiguities in the crucial "adverse impact" provisions evidently are deliberate, intended to afford EEOC the opportunity to embark upon an enforcement approach different from that followed by the other agencies. If this occurs, then employers will continue to be confronted with conflicting interpretations of their obligations despite the claimed uniformity in the official "guidelines" of the federal enforcement agencies.

NOTES

1. Order of Willard Wirtz, Secretary of Labor, "Validation of Employment Tests by Contractors and Subcontractors Subject to the Provisions of Executive Order 11246," 33 Fed. Reg. 14392 (September 24, 1968).

2. In sworn testimony their chief author, the late Dr. William Enneis of the EEOC, denied any such intent.

3. "Differential.validity" refers to the possibility that the same test will predict in a different manner for one racial or sexual subgroup than another.

4. 29 C.F.R. § 1607.5(a).

5. E.g., compare *Douglas v. Hampton*, 512 F.2d 976, 984-85 (D.C. Cir. 1975), with *Vulcan Society v. Civil Service Comm'n*, 490 F.2d 387 (2d Cir. 1973).

6. For example, the employer might check the reading difficulty level of training materials to make certain they are no more difficult than the materials an employee will actually read on the job.

Networking: The New Way to Find Female and Minority Managers

Darlene Orlov

What happens when a company makes a genuine commitment to promote EEO—but the applicants don't appear? Suppose you have developed an acceptable affirmative action program. Your managers and supervisors have been trained in EEO compliance, and perhaps you even included EEO action as part of their performance appraisal system. Your company offers high salaries and excellent career opportunities, and your benefits package is outstanding. Yet despite all your efforts, you still have not been able to increase the proportion of females and minorities among your employees. And the number of your female and minority managers remains discouragingly low. Where are the applicants? How can you reach them?

Limitations of Traditional Recruiting Methods

A company cannot hire, and eventually promote, females and minorities unless such individuals apply for employment. To increase

---

Darlene Orlov is president of Orlov Resources for Business, a human resources consulting firm in New York City that specializes in management training, employee communications, EEO compliance, and employee selection.

the proportion of women and minorities at the management level, applicant flow at all levels must be increased substantially. But this has been a problem for many organizations.

The difficulty can stem from many sources. Often companies project an unattractive image to female and minority applicants, even if official policy encourages their recruitment. And traditional avenues of solicitation are often limited in their effectiveness. The three established methods of increasing applicant flow—advertisements, employment agencies, and search firms—can work extremely well for companies seeking only a few applicants; but often they do not yield a large pool of women and minorities.

Agencies and search firms have traditionally been geared to finding the white male manager—the manager most desired in the pre-EEO past. Some agencies lack experience in interviewing and recruiting from other populations, and they suffer from a popular image identifying them with the white male establishment. While a few agencies and search firms are specializing today in minorities and women, there is no guarantee that your preferred applicant—or the best applicants in general—seek out such specialized help.

In addition, by their very nature, these traditional methods are indirect. Newspaper advertisements must be "blind"—sex and minority status cannot be mentioned. Employers are also prohibited by law from asking agencies and search firms to send them applicants of a specific sex or minority group.

The chief weakness of traditional recruitment methods, however, is even more basic. In using these techniques, you are competing directly with every other organization seeking management talent. There is no way for you to demonstrate the particular benefits of employment with your company, the special encouragement you are offering to women and minorities, your excellent track record in promoting such individuals from within the ranks: in short, how much you want to hire, train, and promote that talented applicant. Most companies today have affirmative action plans and seek qualified female and minority managers. Your message can be lost in the shuffle, because you cannot beam it directly at those individuals you want to reach.

Increasing Applicant Flow: A New Solution

The key to generating increased applicant flow is publicity and personal contact with the specific resource groups in which you are interested. And the place to begin is at home, in your own organization.

First, you must carefully analyze your company's reputation among the desired groups. This is your market research, your public opinion survey, the necessary preliminary to developing a plan and implementing it. Such an analysis can be accomplished by consulting community leaders, officers of organizations composed of or concerned with minorities and women, and college alumni officers. Even more important, raise the issue with your own employees. Your public relations department will be aware of any particular problems within the community that would affect your reputation as an employer. Once aware of the problem—it might be as simple as poor public transportation to your plant, or as touchy as memories of a long-discontinued discriminatory hiring practice—you can take steps to solve it by recasting your organization's image in a more positive light.

The Networking Concept

Once aware of your organization's reputation as an employer, you can involve your own employees in recruitment. Make every effort to tap into existing associations. Your successful female and minority managers know other successful or potentially successful managers, people like themselves who are motivated, talented, and often members of the same sex or ethnic group. Minorities and women will tend to know more minority and female individuals than do most of your white male managers and personnel staff. They may belong to the same professional associations, be neighbors, have served as volunteers together, have gone to the same college, or simply socialize together. But whatever the basis for the relationship, it is a valuable source of new applicants for your organization.

To gain access to this network of contacts—similar to the traditional network operating for white males—several approaches should be used simultaneously. It is absolutely necessary to try various methods to increase applicant flow through the network concept. The strength of this concept is that it gives the company access to the most diverse population of applicants, personally recommended by employees whose successful performance is established. But because of this diversity, different methods will be required to reach all the employees.

Spotlight Existing Success Stories

Step one in the networking approach to recruiting is to identify the successful minority and female employees in your organization, particularly those at the management level or of potential management caliber. It often is helpful to spotlight such individuals in any case —as evidence of your seriousness about affirmative action. But this must not be done in a patronizing way, or in a style that suggests tokenism. One black or female face in a recruitment brochure is better than none, but it is not enough to persuade such individuals to apply.

Gain Confidence of Employees and Applicants

Your next step is the most crucial, and the most difficult, but it will pay off not only in a larger pool of qualified applicants but in generally improved morale and a stronger organization. You must gain the confidence of your minority and female employees, and through them, of potential applicants in their networks. You must convince them of your company's sincerity about hiring more people like themselves; and you must persuade them that you have made a genuine commitment to train and promote such individuals from within the organization.

Begin by increasing employee awareness of your affirmative action activities. Although the government requires employers to allow employees to have access to the affirmative action plan, very few request to see it. Many workers know of their employer's policies only through a brief memo or a government poster. Publicize your plan through the company newspaper, more extensive memos, and meetings, especially question-and-answer sessions. The affirmative action plan offers an excellent opportunity to focus employee attention on EEO problems and issues, to generate discussion, and to begin a dialogue that can involve selected employees in your recruiting efforts. But remember that sincerity is the key. Women and minorities are often extremely sensitive to sugarcoating of problems; they will not volunteer to recruit applicants unless they are convinced that your company is serious about affirmative action.

There are a variety of ways to demonstrate your commitment. First, be prepared to approach individual employees openly and directly: "We want to hire more people like you. We need your help in identifying applicants." You will use these individuals as salespeople for your organization.

Next, call a meeting to be led by a senior-level personnel professional, preferably the facility or company EEO officer. Invite every female and minority employee holding a position in a classification where you want more female and minority applicants. Explain your commitment to EEO, and be specific about how your employees can help act as a resource to increase female and minority employment. Be prepared to suggest a variety of types of involvement and have a follow-up mechanism planned, such as a second meeting, a committee, or a series of individual conferences.

Examine Your Track Record

Such a meeting, of course, should involve two-way communication. It offers a chance to learn your employees' opinions on affirmative action in general, and your track record in particular. It is this pattern of accomplishment—what you have done for women and minorities, and what you currently are doing—that will convince applicants to contact you. If your record to date is inadequate, consisting chiefly of statements and objectives, begin at once to plan concrete programs. Consider promoting from within—examine your employee roster and search out individuals who may have been overlooked in the past. It may be necessary to re-examine some advancement policies for the short term.

Encourage Professional Development

Specific programs can include training, both in-house and out; special films and guest speakers; tuition reimbursement; special seminars in professional development; opportunities to observe the functions of other departments and divisions through interdepartmental meetings, plant tours, and week-long job exchanges; support groups for women and minorities in special jobs, such as those that involve extensive field work and client contact; and improved orientation for new employees. In some cases, remedial training programs can have a real impact, educating an entire community about your company's willingness to recruit females and minorities. Word of mouth will communicate your sincerity about affirmative action, but such programs should also be publicized and featured in recruitment presentations.

Encourage your employees to join professional associations and to become active in them. Many employees at the supervisor level are unaware that such opportunities exist. And women and minorities, traditionally excluded from membership in some prestigious professional groups, may also be unaware of the many organizations that now welcome their participation. Your company should pay for professional memberships and sponsor attendance at conferences. This helps to develop potential managers, and will also give your company favorable exposure. Such involvement broadens the network of contacts of your female and minority employees; and in the long run, it will help them help you find the applicants you seek.

Employees should also be encouraged to attend conventions and meetings and to become involved in community activities. Often such involvement is perceived as conflicting with the commitment to the employer, particularly at the supervisor level. Your female or minority employees may need some release time in order to participate, and it is likely that they will require reassurance that your company really appreciates the value of these "extracurricular" activities.

But remember that such committed, active individuals are very effective spokespeople for your organization. They are advertisements for the success of your affirmative action policies and the comfortable climate your organization offers to women and minorities. A successful female or minority manager is a persuasive recruitment tool who can speak with conviction to groups within the company about any new policies or opportunities. Such a spokesperson can also carry your message to groups on the outside, formally or informally. You may want to ask individuals or a special committee to serve as a liaison with alumni and college groups, to speak on campuses or at local high schools, or to participate in developing recruitment materials aimed at special groups.

The Nature of Networks

Having laid the groundwork, developed special programs, and targeted and contacted a key group of women and minority employees, how do you actually recruit more applicants? Where will they come from?

As will be clear by now, "networking" is merely a new word describing a very old sort of relationship—the continuous social and professional linkage between individuals. Networking is the most natural of recruitment methods, because the aims of the network are the same as that of the employer—making contacts for employment, matching qualified individuals with appealing jobs. Networking is the most traditional method of recruitment as well: an estimated 80 percent of job openings are filled through word of mouth and personal contacts.

As traditionally used, networking seems almost effortless, so accustomed are employers to soliciting and accepting referrals. But this method has been used chiefly to identify white male "majority" applicants. Their networks are well known and accepted by employers and applicants alike. The tie-ins between a largely white male managerial staff and a host of similar managers at other companies are well established.

It is a different story, however, with women and minorities. Their networks are also strong, but they are less familiar to business, and perhaps less consciously professionally oriented. In the past, many women and minorities were reluctant to use their contacts to further their careers, or were simply unaware that they could do so. Now, however, women and minorities are becoming aware of the usefulness of contacts and of their legitimacy. Some new organizations have arisen specifically to provide a forum for discussion and establishment of relationships among minority and female professionals.

Like traditional white male networks, the new female and minority networks offer a broad base of contacts. Networks are parallel, with individuals in one job classification acquainted with others in the same classification or rank within the company or in other organizations. They are also vertical: minority and female employees often are more likely to know other minorities and females even at much higher or lower positions in the corporate hierarchy than are their white male counterparts. Networks also extend into related fields, with a purchasing officer knowing salespeople and their administrative staffs, or a woman engineer knowing a woman in marketing or industrial design. Often it is the most upwardly mobile individuals who are the most tuned in to the existence of these networks and the most willing to use them to recruit new applicants.

But to actually tap into these networks, it is necessary to ask for assistance, to be frank about the company's problems in recruiting women and minorities. If you have established that you are committed to affirmative action, you should be able to extend your applicant pool significantly through involving your employees in the search. The payoff can be great, for such applicants come personally recommended by your own successful employees. And the reputation of your organization as an equal opportunity employer will soon become well established.

Data Processing: A Tool for EEO Compliance

Farrell E. Bloch

The equal employment opportunity regulations of the sixties and seventies created the need for a new type of personnel manager: the equal employment officer. Like other personnel professionals such as compensation analysts and employment test examiners, EEO officers must manage a good deal of quantitative information. Much of the quantitative work is easy but tedious—for example, simply counting the numbers of individuals employed in various occupations. Other aspects of the work can be difficult—for example, the availability analysis required by the Office of Federal Contract Compliance Programs. Fortunately, however, affirmative action officers can now use computers to alleviate these and other burdens.

One basic task of an EEO officer is the construction of an affirmative action plan. These plans have three components:

(1) an availability analysis—an assessment of the numbers of females and minorities among those qualified and available for certain jobs;

Farrell Bloch is cofounder of Econometric Research, Inc., a consulting firm based in Washington, D.C. Dr. Bloch has testified as an expert labor economist and statistician in several employment discrimination cases and has helped companies prepare affirmative action plans.

(2) a utilization analysis—a comparison between the numbers of females and minorities actually employed and the benchmarks determined by the availability analysis; and

(3) the establishment of goals and timetables for the hiring of females and minorities in jobs in which they are underutilized.

Although the availability analysis must be done by hand, much of the utilization analysis and the establishment of goals and timetables can be performed on the computer. This, of course, may be small comfort to those whose main concern, in light of the often ambiguous government guidelines, is developing an availability analysis.

Modification of Existing System

If a company uses a computer to keep personnel records for payroll or other purposes, it should cost little extra to modify the data processing system to accommodate EEO analysis. This accommodation basically involves maintaining additional information about employees, such as sex, race, specific job, recruitment source, and previous work experience. Information such as recruitment source and previous work experience can be coded. For example, recruitment source can be classified into such categories as employee referral, private employment agency, and newspaper advertisement. Similarly, previous experience can be classified into number of years worked as a clerical, salesperson, and operative.

The level of detail of these categorizations can be specified by the affirmative action officer. It may be desirable to code which employment agency referred the employees—some may be better than others for finding qualified females and minorities. Similarly, for some purposes, occupational classifications more detailed than the basic EEO categories are required. For example, outside sales experience may be much more important than retail sales experience in analyzing qualifications for sales jobs in the wholesale trades.

Much of the information needed for affirmative action analysis may already be kept in computer files. Examples are dates of hire and rates of compensation. Unfortunately, compensation data in payroll records may not be of much use to EEO officers. For year-end tax calculations, payroll files typically keep individuals' annual earnings. However, the rate of compensation—hourly wage or weekly salary—usually is a better indicator of an employee's status and upward mobility in a firm and therefore more suitable for EEO purposes.

To illustrate the advantage of compensation rates over annual earnings, consider an employee earning $5.00 an hour in 1979 and $6.00 an hour in 1980. Suppose that in 1979, this individual worked 2,000 hours at the $5.00 rate and 200 overtime hours at the $7.50 "time-and-a-half" rate. Total 1979 earnings are therefore 2,000 (5.00) + 200 (7.50) = $11,500. Suppose further that in 1980, business slows down: not only is overtime no longer required, but also temporary layoffs are necessary. As a result, this employee works only 1,800 hours in 1980. Total 1980 earnings of 1,800 (6.00) = $10,800 are less than 1979 earnings of $11,500 and clearly do not indicate the employee's 20 percent promotion in hourly pay between 1979 and 1980.

This basic policy of adding employee characteristics to an already existing computer file is easy to execute. All that need be done is to discuss with data processing analysts the information to be added and the exact way in which it should be coded. Because there is no reason why computer programmers and systems analysts should know anything about EEO, it is best to give them very detailed instructions. It is also a good idea to tell them exactly how the data will be used, in what format any computer output would be most convenient, and how often the files will be updated, the data analyzed, and reports written. Updating can be scheduled to precede report writing, and the format of the computer output can be designed to fit the purpose of the reports.

Interaction between affirmative action and data processing personnel can be difficult if each side is not sensitive to the differences in the other's training and experience. Avoiding EEO jargon and sparing no detail in data processing requests are the best preventative medicine for possible communication problems.

Adding an affirmative action function to the data processing department costs little because, very simply, the basic computer system, including personnel, already exists. Thus, including an affirmative action function is like mining a bit more ore from a working mine: the major costs already have been incurred.

It is difficult to imagine in 1980 many firms or institutions that are large enough to have an EEO obligation yet are completely without data processing support. (Data processing services provided from the outside—for payroll or other reasons—can also be used for EEO functions.) If no data processing capability is present, the cost of establishing it for EEO work can be considerable—rather like opening a new mine than mining ore from an existing one. The benefits to EEO officers of computerizing employment information perhaps will be less than company costs of establishing the computerized system from scratch. However, technological advances and consequent price reductions in the computer industry continue to reduce these costs.

Benefits of Computerized Systems

What are the benefits of a computerized EEO system? First, such a system obviates the need for some clerical support—thereby lowering company costs. Second, all tabulations done by computer will be arithmetically correct—assuming, of course, reliable input data and competent programming. This situation is clearly superior to having, say, clerical employees who always hated math do the same work. Third, the computer, by retaining information, eases a paperwork and storage burden. Fourth, and perhaps most important, the computer can perform statistical analyses needed for affirmative action plans, compliance reviews, and the relatively rare but crucial discrimination suit involving pattern-and-practice allegations.

An affirmative action plan's utilization analysis is one function whose burden the computer can help reduce. The courts have recognized that disparities between the percentages of females or minorities available for work in a given labor market and the percentage of these protected class members hired or employed are not always significant; in many cases, the courts have adopted statistical guidelines to determine when it is significant. The basic idea is to ascertain how likely it would be for, say, a certain number of clericals in a firm to be black, given the availability of blacks in the labor market from which clericals are drawn. For example, if 20 percent of the source labor market is black and a firm hires 19 black out of 100 total clericals, such a practice would generally be considered consistent with equal opportunity hiring. However, if only 7 of the 100 clericals were black, the disparity between 7 of 100 and 20 percent would be considered statistically significant.

An analogy may be helpful here. Suppose we were interested in testing whether a coin is fair, that is, whether it is equally likely to come up "heads" as "tails." We flip the coin 100 times, expecting something like (but not necessarily exactly) 50 heads and 50 tails. Statisticians can compute the probability that any number of heads turns up. It is possible, although not likely, that, if the coin were fair, we would get 90 heads and 10 tails. A more plausible explanation of this result is that the coin is not fair, that it is more likely to come up heads than tails. Statisticians can help to decide between a conclusion that the coin is fair and the conclusion that heads are more likely than tails. A result of 52 heads, like the above result of 19 black clericals, would generally be deemed consistent with a fair coin or a nondiscriminatory hiring practice. A result of 90 heads, like the result of 7 black clericals, could still occur with a fair coin or a nondiscriminatory hiring practice, but the probability of occurrence, by chance, is so small that one generally would conclude instead that the coin is not fair, or that the net effect of the hiring practice is to exclude blacks from clerical jobs.

If certain job groups indicate underutilization of female and minority workers, EEO agencies may require the establishment of goals and timetables to correct the disparities. As in pinpointing any underutilization, data processing and statistical skills can be of help here as well. By noting retirements (from records on the age of employees) and by assuming patterns of other dimensions of turnover, one can forecast the number of openings in various jobs and help to project opportunities for female and minority hires and promotions. With a computer, it is easy to perform a sensitivity analysis, that is, to determine how the number of prospective job openings changes when turnover assumptions are altered.

If records are kept on applicants as well as employees, and on various employee selection criteria such as education requirements and employer-administered tests, then one can analyze which selection criteria, if any, are disproportionately excluding members of protected classes. Federal selection guidelines require that if the female or minority pass rate on a test or other selection criterion is less than 80 percent of the male or white pass rate, then that selection criterion must be validated, that is, shown to be related to the job for which it is used. For example, if 30 percent of blacks and 60 percent of whites pass a written employment exam, the 80 percent rule is violated, because the black pass rate is less than 80 percent of the white pass rate: $30\% \div 60\% = 50\%$ is less than 80%. Computer programmers can easily compute these relative pass rates and indicate where the 80 percent rule is violated. If instructed, systems analysts can look at this issue for specific groups of applicants or limited time periods and can analyze the joint effect of two or more selection criteria.

Although much of the emphasis of government compliance officers is on hiring, wage disparities are becoming the focus of an increasing number of compliance investigations and discrimination charges. However, not all wage disparities are evidence of discrimination. Females may be paid less than males because they have less seniority, tend to apply for lower paying jobs, or do not bid for promotions as frequently as males. Detailed computer files permit an analysis of the extent to which wage disparities can be attributed to these explanatory variables. The remaining unexplained wage disparities are the result of factors not explicitly accounted for, only one of which is discrimination. Back-pay claims are often based on a naive comparison of simple wage differentials. With more detailed wage analysis, back-pay liability can often be shown to be much smaller than alleged, and in some cases, nonexistent.

Tool for Internal Policy

Although most of the computer applications discussed so far are responses to external demands—government requirements or unfair employment practice allegations—computerized employee files can be of great help for internal affirmative action policy. Data on recruitment source can indicate to EEO directors where outreach activities for qualified females and minorities have proved fruitful. Perhaps one employment agency has referred most black administrators. Data on previous work experience of successful employees can indicate the type of individuals for whom to search. For example, females with previous experience operating office machines may have been easily trainable for certain craft jobs and may have done these jobs well. Results like this can be derived from statistical analysis of previous work experience and such indicators of job success as passing a training course, obtaining high supervisors' ratings, and receiving large and/or frequent promotions.

The analysis of recruitment source and previous work experience can be limited to printing out tabulations indicating, say, how many female managers were referred by employment agency X and how many Hispanic professionals answered newspaper ad Y. It can also involve sophisticated statistical analyses that yield conclusions such as "a thirty-year-old female clerical with a high school diploma and four years of office machine experience has an 82 percent chance of successfully completing our skilled crafts training program." The utilization, selection criteria, and wage analysis discussed above have similar wide ranges of possible complexity.

The important point, though, is that an EEO officer need have no knowledge of statistics or even of data processing to benefit from these or other analyses. All that is needed is clear communication from the EEO officer to data processing personnel (and, possibly, economists or statisticians directing the analysis) on what data are available and what questions would be useful to answer. Clear communication in the other direction to explain computer capabilities and results of any analysis is equally necessary. Prior to all this, however, is an understanding and appreciation that the computer's considerable capacity for the storage, retrieval, and processing of information can be easily harnessed for the use of EEO officers.

JOB EVALUATION

Job Evaluation Systems
and the Changing Law

John V. Harper

In the last half century, the evaluation of jobs has become an increasingly important business activity. Prudent businessmen and managers have learned through experience that sound and productive relationships with employees are built upon the foundation of a fair day's pay for a fair day's work. Though such aspects as prestige and fulfillment are important to the overall job satisfaction of the employee, pay is still the overriding factor: unless employees believe they are fairly compensated for their work, morale problems are inevitable.

In assessing the value of jobs, employers quickly learned they had to consider the fair market value of a job as determined by labor availability, but also the relative value of jobs as compared within the employer's workplace. Not only would punch press operators, for example, wish to be paid at least the going rate for punch press operators in the general work force, but they would also want to be paid more than persons performing less demanding tasks; and they would expect to be paid less than those performing more demanding tasks.

Managers began to search out techniques that would accurately assess the value of jobs. Job evaluation systems, more and more man-

John V. Harper is labor law attorney for the Kellogg Company in Battle Creek, Michigan.

agers found, were the answer. These systems, often professionally applied, provide a systematic approach to assessing the market value of jobs as well as the relative value of jobs. Yet these systems, for all their benefits, are a source of potential litigation for businesses.

Job Evaluation Systems

There are four main types of job evaluation systems currently in use. The simplest and least costly is the ranking system. This system works best when only a small number of jobs is evaluated and when the persons doing the evaluation are familiar with all the jobs. Essentially, ranking requires that key jobs, from the group of jobs to be evaluated, be established and ranked according to value. The pay rates for these key jobs should be in line with the going rate for similar jobs in the marketplace.

Once the key jobs have been determined and ranked, other jobs are compared and valued relative to the key jobs. Usually a pair of jobs is compared at one time, with as many as four persons doing the comparison and evaluation. The results are compared and averaged, and a final value is assigned to each job.

More difficult is the predetermined grading evaluation system, also called the classification system, which is used most frequently by government employers. This system requires that job grades be defined ranging from the simplest, least demanding level to the complex and highly demanding level. Each job level is described, in detail, in such terms as difficulty of work, use of independent judgment, training, character of supervision, responsibility, and leadership. Jobs are compared with the definitions and placed in the level corresponding most closely to the requirements of the job.

The two remaining systems are those most frequently used by private employers. Both are more difficult than the systems just described; each is useful in valuing jobs in complex organizations and in minimizing biases of the raters.

The older of the two is the factor comparison system. Its application begins with the selection of key jobs whose relative values are easily agreed on and whose pay rates are in line with those generally paid in the marketplace. These key jobs are then analyzed in terms of factors, such as skill, mental demand, physical demand, responsibility, and working conditions; the value of the job is apportioned among these factors. For example, if Job A has a value of X, then as apportioned among the factors, 30 percent of Job A may be skill, 30 percent mental demand, 10 percent physical demand, 15 percent responsibility, and 15 percent working conditions.

Other jobs are then compared, by factor, to the key jobs, and a weighted value is determined. Valuing of both key jobs and other jobs can be done in terms of money or points. Use of points is often preferable because it limits the biases that sometimes attend money valuations. Valuations of jobs in points may be converted to a money value by a simple formula.

The last, and most widely used, system is point rating. By far the most complex system, point rating requires the selection of several factors, such as accuracy, aptitude, job knowledge, leadership, manual skill, precision, exertion, memory, strength, mental stability, quality, safety, clothing spoilage, and many others. Because of the variety of factor combinations possible with this system, jobs of similar nature are grouped and valued according to a set of factors selected for that group. Following their selection, the factors are weighted. The relative importance of one factor versus another must be ascertained and assigned a percentage weight. These percentage weights become the basis for assigning points to the various levels within each factor. For example, if job knowledge is weighted at 10 percent, then within that factor, points ranging from 5 to 25, in increments of 5 points, may be assigned to the various levels of job knowledge required. Some jobs, therefore, might have a job knowledge worth 25 points, and these 25 points will be equal to 10 percent of the value of the job. Other jobs may be worth fewer job knowledge points, with the percentage value of job knowledge thereby diminished.

In sum, the various job evaluation systems reflect different degrees of complexity and flexibility. They present different bases for comparing jobs, and these differences render each system more or less vulnerable to attack in any given employment environment.

Legal Environment

Recently, the Department of Labor (DOL) and the Equal Employment Opportunity Commission (EEOC) have shown interest in job evaluation systems. They are particularly interested in whether such systems discriminate against women by unreasonably attributing lesser value to the activities normally performed by women as compared to the activities normally performed by men. The DOL and the EEOC are taking the position that jobs of comparable worth to an employer should be paid the same wage. In particular, if an employer has a job traditionally held by females and another traditionally held by males, and these jobs are of comparable worth, then the employer's failure to pay the same wage for these jobs is discrimination on the basis of sex, in violation of Executive Order 11246 or of Title VII of the Civil Rights Acts of 1964.

The most recent decision by a federal court on the issue of job comparability and sex discrimination is *Lemons v. City & County of Denver*. The plaintiff claimed that her employer maintained a job evaluation system that undervalued the worth of nurses as compared to other jobs predominantly held by males. She further claimed that the undervaluation resulted from a discriminatory application of the evaluation system, and that considered as a whole, the evaluation system had a discriminatory impact on women.

The case arose under both the U.S. Constitution and Title VII. After rejecting the plaintiff's claims under the Constitution, the court addressed the Title VII issues. First it recognized that women have been, and continue to be, discriminated against in employment; and then it held that Congress did not intend to provide a remedy for discrimination claims founded on a job comparability argument.

The court attached great significance to the fact that section 703(h) of Title VII contains a sentence, commonly known as the Bennett Amendment, which provides:

> It shall not be an unlawful employment practice under this title for any employer to differentiate upon the basis of sex in determining the amount of the wages or compensation paid or to be paid to employees of such employer if such differentiation is authorized by the provisions of section 6(d) of the Fair Labor Standards Act of 1939, as amended.

The Court interpreted this amendment to mean that no successful claim against a wage differential based on sex can be maintained under Title VII unless that claim can be successfully maintained under the Equal Pay Act.

Actually, the court in *Lemons* was in harmony with a number of prior cases that have held, with varying degrees of explicitness, that jobs must be more than comparable to one another for the comparisons under the Equal Pay Act.[2] The Equal Pay Act prohibits pay differences based on sex if the jobs are equal. The Act provides that equality of jobs will be tested on the basis of skill, effort, and responsibility performed under similar working conditions; courts have interpreted this test to mean substantial equality in these factors.

Notwithstanding *Lemons* and its predecessors, the DOL and the EEOC are pursuing the job comparability issue. The DOL, for example, has instituted debarment proceedings against at least two government contractors, challenging their job evaluation systems as discriminatory on the basis of sex.[3] The DOL alleges, essentially, that the defendants have instituted job evaluation systems that undervalue tasks performed by women and overvalue those performed by men. The DOL claims that it may successfully challenge such evaluation systems under the Executive Order because that Order does not contain the limiting Bennett Amendment language and because the Executive Order specifically prohibits discrimination based on sex.

For its part, the EEOC takes the position that the Bennett Amendment applies only where jobs of similar content are being compared, and that the amendment does not act to limit the broad language of section 703(a)(2), which prohibits discrimination based on sex. Though not announced officially, the EEOC position has been announced unofficially by its vice-chairman, Daniel Leach.

In statements before the Federal Bar Association on June 9, 1978, Commissioner Leach outlined patterns and statistics that he said demonstrate that the status of women in employment has not changed significantly since the passage of Title VII. This situation is largely due, he maintained, to continued class-wide discrimination against women for job and wage opportunities. He cited, among other things, that the ratio of women's to men's pay from 1960 to 1975 has remained almost constant, at approximately 60 percent. He also stated that even when analyzed by occupations, women earn considerably less than men in the same occupations.

In suggesting how to deal with these statistics, Commissioner Leach states:

> First of all we've got to face this fact: as long as jobs traditionally held by women are assigned less value than those traditionally held by men, the earning picture for women will remain grim. Some people are beginning to recognize the limiting and confining nature of the concept *"equal pay* for *equal work"* and are beginning to talk about "equal pay for work of equal value." [emphasis in text]

Commissioner Leach disclosed that the EEOC has entered into a two-year contract with the National Academy of Science to assess the feasibility of developing objective and comprehensive methods of determining job comparability. The DOL, for its part, has entered into a contract with the academy to evaluate the usefulness of a functional job analysis system on which the government's Dictionary of Occupational Titles is based.

Though the courts have thus far rejected the job comparability test suggested by the DOL and the EEOC, the importance of these agencies' positions should not be treated lightly. The DOL position is important because the agency can seek imposition of penalties through an administrative procedure and from administrative law judges who may be more sympathetic to the DOL position than the courts have been. Furthermore, the EEOC has never articulated its position before the courts. Individual plaintiffs have raised the comparability issue, and in each case, these plaintiffs tended to mount feeble and sometimes indirect assaults on behalf of a job comparability standard. The EEOC may well be much better prepared before a court.

Relevance to Job Evaluation Systems

Many experts in the job evaluation field maintain that, properly applied, job evaluation systems do not discriminate on any impermissible grounds and that these systems provide rational and fairly objective methods of evaluating jobs. When a system seems to discriminate in pay on the basis of sex, many experts blame a faulty application of the system.

Certainly, an employer must exercise great care in the application of any job evaluation system. Employers should seek to avoid ad hoc modifications of job evaluation systems or shortcuts that tend to affect the integrity of the systems. These activities make any subsequent valuation of jobs suspect and may even expose the employer to liability under the Equal Pay Act standard. Yet even when application of a job evaluation system is proper, each type of system has its own inherent susceptibilities to undervaluing of jobs performed by females. Recognition of these susceptibilities is important.

In the ranking system, where jobs are compared as whole entities, sex-based stereotypes may influence the decisions of the raters, especially if all the raters are male. A similar potential exists with respect to the predetermined grading evaluation system. Jobs under this system are treated as whole entities, too, and are paid in accordance with their difficulty and need for judgmental ability. Again, there is a significant risk that all male raters may tend to see jobs performed by females as being relatively simpler and less judgmental than those performed by men.

These kinds of failings are less likely to occur in the factor and point systems. Neither of these systems evaluates jobs as whole entities; rather, the various factors of the job are analyzed and valued. Thus, errors in judgment may be offset. For example, under a factor system evaluation, a sex-based assumption that undervalues the skill portion of a job traditionally held by females may overvalue the working conditions factor. Similarly, the undervaluation-overvaluation pairing could occur under the point system where, for instance, the factors of precision and leadership are considered.

Employers should pay attention to situations that warn of possible misapplication of a job evaluation system. Close scrutiny is called for if an employer notices that all, or almost all, of the jobs held by females are paid rates less than all, or almost all, jobs held by males. Scrutiny is especially required if all the raters under the evaluation system are male. Scrutiny is called for, too, when the pay rate for a particular traditionally female job is less than that generally paid by competitors for similar jobs.

When valuing jobs in the professional and managerial areas, employers should take particular care. If they use the point system, they should recognize that within factors such as aptitude, leadership, and mental ability, gradations for the awarding of points may be somewhat arbitrary and difficult to justify. Unless very careful analysis and development of these gradations within factors is done, the resultant job evaluation system may be open to serious challenge where it impacts adversely upon females.

As a final measure, employers should consider some training in equal employment opportunity law for all raters and managers of a job evaluation system, and employers should insure that females are a part of the evaluation system, both as raters and as managers.

Conclusion

The issue of equal pay for comparable jobs is still in its infancy. At present, the courts reject, as a matter of law, the notion that comparable jobs deserve equal pay, and they have refused to apply any standard for measuring the equality of jobs other than on the basis of similar job content and substantially equal skill, effort, and responsibility. Nonetheless, the positions of the DOL and EEOC indicate the direction these agencies are taking for enforcement of the federal civil rights laws. Employers may properly prepare themselves for future developments in the job comparability area by giving careful attention to the management and application of job evaluation systems.

NOTES

1. 17 FEP Cases 906 (D.C. Colo. 1978).

2. *Angelo v. Bacharach Instrument Co.*, 555 F.2d 1164 (3rd Cir. 1977); *Brennan v. City Stores*, 497 F.2d 235 (5th Cir. 1973); *Brennan v. Prince William Hospital Corp.*, 503 F.2d 282 (4th Cir. 1974); *Wetzel v. Liberty Mutual Insurance Co.*, 449 F. Supp. 397 (W.D. Pa. 1978).

3. The names of the contractors are withheld, as the proceedings are not yet a matter of public record.

Auditing Your Job Evaluation Plan—A Case Study

Catherine M. Meek

Is equal pay for equal work an illusory concept? The Equal Pay Act prohibits pay discrimination because of sex; Title VII of the Civil Rights Act of 1964 prohibits pay discrimination on the basis of race, color, religion, sex, or national origin; and the Age Discrimination in Employment Act prohibits pay discrimination against persons between the ages of 40 and 70. Yet pay discrimination still exists.

Most organizations have established formal programs to foster equitable treatment for all employees. However, a company's good intentions or stated policy of having a nondiscriminatory compensation system are of little significance unless the system actually results in equal pay for equal work.

To determine how much to pay people, most employers have instituted formal job evaluation systems designed to measure and reward the relative value of positions within their organizations. Some of the key characteristics of most job evaluation plans are that they:

- compare jobs, one with another;
- incorporate the judgment of the rater; and
- presumably measure job content and responsibility.

Catherine M. Meek is a principal in the Philadelphia consulting office of Towers, Perrin, Forster & Crosby, Inc., specializing in compensation and equal employment opportunity.

Cathy J. Raphael, a senior research specialist with Towers, Perrin, Forster & Crosby in New York City, assisted in the preparation of this article.

From an equal pay perspective, two major problems of these plans are that (1) although controlled, there is a heavy dependence on the judgment of the rater, both in the design and administration of the plan, and (2) generally there is limited *direct* association with objective, quantifiable position criteria.

Evaluate Your Evaluation System

It may be desirable to analyze your evaluation system—not only to ensure that it is *not* fostering discriminatory pay practices, but also to determine whether employees are actually being paid on the bases that the plan purports to measure. Towers, Perrin, Forster & Crosby was recently asked to undertake such an assignment for a company that used a point-factor system to evaluate its middle management positions.

Use of multiple regression techniques[1] enabled us to isolate the actual determinations of pay. We could then discern whether suspect characteristics—for example, age or sex—influenced the variances in employees' pay.

Analysis of a Point-Factor Plan

In establishing internal pay equity, a properly designed point-factor plan should include only those factors that represent discrete entities. In other words, one factor should not be measured by any other factor. Instead, different "pieces" of a position should be measured separately, then added together to determine the relative value of the position. Thus, no (or little) correlation should exist between any two factors or between any factor and the total points accorded to a position.

In our recent assignment, the company's plan purported to evaluate jobs on the bases of:
- Education and Experience
- Analytical Complexity
- Organization Accountability (as measured by the size of the unit)
- Management Responsibility (as measured by number of employees and size of payroll supervised)
- Contacts.

In analyzing this plan, we first asked: "Are the five major factors actually measuring five different position criteria? Which factors are most significant?"

Using the actual factor-by-factor evaluations, we correlated the points assigned to each factor with the total points for the positions. We found that only two factors were actually being measured, with the highest correlation between Organization Accountability and total points. We observed that Organization Accountability accounted for over 93 percent of the variance in points. When Analytical Complexity was added to our model, we could explain an additional 6 percent. In other words, by taking the point scores under these *two* factors alone, we could predict with 99 percent accuracy the total point score that would result from the application of all *five* factors.

What Do the Two Factors Actually Measure?

Having determined that there were really only two major factors at work in the evaluation plan, we wanted to identify in hard, numerical data what those factors were measuring about the positions. To accomplish this, we gathered specific, quantifiable data covering functional, organizational, and supervisory aspects of the positions, as well as job evaluation points. These data included:

- Job Family (e.g., Finance, Personnel)
- Reporting Level (a numerical variable that reveals a company's organizational structure)
- Number of Exempt Employees Supervised
- Size of Unit (revenues)
- Education (years of schooling)
- Age
- Length of Company Service
- Sex
- Time in Position.

The total point scores were then regressed against all these numerical data for each position. Where there is, in fact, a statistical relationship between these measures and the total point scores, we can conclude that the measure is a contributor to the point score. Furthermore, we can identify the weighting of that influence.

Table 1, following, illustrates that by knowing the values for the quantitative measures listed above, we could replicate, with 95 percent accuracy, the total point scores actually produced by the job evaluation plan.

173

Table 1
Point Score Analysis

Quantitative Measure	Weight
Reporting Level	93.5%
Job Family	0.9
Number of Exempt Employees Supervised	0.3
Age	0.2
Total:	94.9%

What Are the Actual Determinants of Employees' Pay?

Now that we could identify and weight the objective measures inherent in the evaluation plan, we wanted to determine if these same measures or factors were being used by management in determining actual pay levels. Additional stepwise multiple regression analyses were therefore performed using the listed quantitative measures. At this stage, *actual* base salaries, rather than the point scores, were used as the dependent variable.

Table 2, following, illustrates the results of this analysis. As can be seen, Reporting Level is still the position measure most highly correlated with pay. However, with the exception of Number of Exempt Employees Supervised, these measures of actual determination of pay were not factors included in the job evaluation plan. Of far greater concern is the fact that pay variances are explained at least in part by a factor—Sex—that should raise a red flag in terms of potential EEO violations.

Table 2
Actual Pay Analysis

Quantitative Measure	Weight
Reporting Level	66.6%
Age	10.3
Length of Company Service	1.1
Job Family	1.0
Size of Unit	2.5
Number of Exempt Employees Supervised	1.2
Sex	0.6
Total:	83.3%

What Do These Quantitative Results Indicate?

The results of our regression analyses confirmed that there were differences between the company's pay "policy" and its pay "practice." Though this situation is hardly unique, such differences do indicate that the compensation system is not rewarding employees according to the objective embodied in the plan's design. Moreover, pay disparities produced by the system could leave the company open to EEO charges.

This type of analysis is a necessary first step. An employer can then decide on a rational and informed basis whether the pay "policy" needs to be redefined. If this is the case, the next task is to decide what factors *should* determine pay. Of course, as discussed in the following section, the factors selected should be only those that can be validated as job-related.

Analysis of Design of Job Evaluation Plan

Historically, the Equal Employment Opportunity Commission (EEOC) and other compliance agencies were primarily (if not exclusively) concerned with whether the *results* of a company's job evaluation system were discriminatory. If pay discrimination was not apparent, little attention was paid to the design or operation of the evaluation system.

However, the EEOC is now questioning whether a job evaluation system itself may contribute to causing or perpetuating pay discrimination. Whether or not the major study in progress by the National Academy of Sciences leads the EEOC to mandate one form of job evaluation or to prohibit the use of another form, it seems clear that systems themselves will no longer be free from official scrutiny.

In view of these developments, it makes sense for an employer to review its job evaluation system for potential discriminatory elements. If a point-factor system is used, each of the component factors should be analyzed to determine if, in fact, it is job-related. Factors such as Education, Experience, and Contacts could pose problems. Courts have held that such criteria should not be used in defining job requirements (for example, for hiring and promotion purposes) unless they can be validated in terms of on-the-job performance.[2] The same caveat should apply to the use of nonvalidated factors in job evaluation plans.

Furthermore, in the quantitative analyses described in the case study, these EEO-suspect factors had no statistically significant influence on either the total evaluation points or pay levels. If, as we suspect, this would be the case in many plans, there is no demonstrable reason for retaining such factors as stated determinants of pay.

Conclusion

No one can guarantee that any job evaluation system is immune from legal challenge. EEO laws do not mandate that employers adopt a particular system, or, in fact, any system. They do, however, state that whatever approach is used cannot result in pay or opportunity discrimination against protected classes of individuals.

Employers would be well advised to audit their job evaluation systems and ensure that:

- positions are evaluated on the basis of job content;
- only objective, job-related factors are used to measure job content;
- factors measure what the organization intends to pay for; and
- subjective elements are eliminated from the plan.

Performing such an audit is by no means a small undertaking. In fact, for many organizations, collecting the necessary background data for multiple regression analysis may in itself prove a formidable task. Yet, a laissez-faire approach may cost considerably more in the long run, both financially and in terms of employee morale.

NOTES

1. The multiple regression modeling described in this article is based on the work of Kenneth E. Foster and Jill Kanin-Lovers, compensation specialists for TPF & C. See, for example, "Determinants of Organizational Pay Policy," *Compensation Review* (Third Quarter 1977).

2. A review of the cases reveals, for example, that Education is difficult to validate as job-related. In two cases where college degree requirements were upheld—for airline pilots in *Spurlock v. United Airlines*, 475 F.2d 216 (10th Cir. 1972) and for hospital laboratory technicians in *Townsend v. Nassau County Medical Center*, 558 F.2d 117 (2d Cir. 1977) *cert. denied*, 1978—the courts emphasized public safety considerations in sustaining the requirements. Such an argument would be difficult to uphold for most white collar positions.

Comparable Pay:
A Management Perspective

Joel H. Kaplan and Richard E. Lieberman

Life, we are reminded, is an underpaid occupation. So too, it is argued, are jobs held predominantly by women. And that contention forms the central core of the comparable worth theory.

Women are underpaid, so the argument runs, in regard to their worth to the employer and, perhaps more critically, underpaid in comparison to jobs predominantly held by men.

There has been an earnings gap between males and females in the workplace since biblical times, when a female worker was worth thirty shekels while a male worker was worth fifty.[1] Today, women in the workplace earn approximately 30 cents for every 50 cents earned by working males. The Equal Employment Opportunity Commission (EEOC) is on the verge of undertaking draconian efforts to eliminate that earnings gap.

"Equal Pay for Equal Work," the movement of the past, involves the Equal Pay Act of 1963's prohibition against paying different wages to male and female workers holding substantially equal jobs. This law is limited to jobs that are virtually identical in content. Supplementing the Equal Pay Act is a new legal thrust with a new slogan: "Equal Pay for Jobs of Comparable Worth." This concept focuses on

Joel H. Kaplan and Richard E. Lieberman are partners with the Chicago office of the Seyfarth, Shaw, Fairweather & Geraldson law firm. They represent management in labor and equal employment opportunity law.

the wage differences between male- and female-held jobs involving entirely different types of work—teachers and cab drivers, electricians and nurses, secretaries and executives, and an endless series of combinations.

In essence, the comparable worth theory argues that through a combination of sex-biased market forces—historical female protective statutes, societal influences, subjective male values, and intentional corporate discrimination—jobs held by women are underpaid compared to jobs held by men. The government and women's groups contend that, to achieve elevation of wages for traditionally female jobs, these inequities can and should be corrected through litigation under various equal employment opportunity statutes and executive orders. This contention forms the basis of the comparable worth theory, described by two EEOC Commissioners as perhaps "the most important issue of the 1980s for minorities and women."

The Underpinnings of the Comparable Worth Theory

Advocates of the comparable worth theory point to a number of reasons for the present pay disparity between male and female workers.

Basic to the theory is the belief that, prior to the Equal Pay Act and Title VII, female compensation reflected various forms of lawful discrimination. Hence, through the operation of protective laws—which may have created an oversupply of women in certain limited occupations—and through just plain employer villainy, women's wages were unnaturally depressed. That Congress dealt with this issue in the Equal Pay Act gives the comparable worth theorists little pause.

The passage of the Equal Pay Act in 1963 and of Title VII of the Civil Rights Act of 1964 has, in their view, brought about few changes. The pre-1963 market price of women's salaries, they say, depresses the current market price. Moreover, because women were barred from access to certain jobs before 1964 and clustered in other occupations, they argue that even today these jobs are viewed as being at the low end of the job hierarchy.

This hierarchical lock-in, they argue, is reinforced by job evaluation systems structured either to reflect the market and hence to preserve the historical low-paid position of women's jobs, or otherwise "rigged" to devalue women's jobs. They contend that, in a job evaluation system, the selection of factors and the weights of these factors determine the ultimate value of the job; women's jobs, they argue, have been rated low because the selection and weighting process has been skewed to favor male jobs. Why, they ask, should physical effort count so much more than mental effort in most job evaluation systems, therefore rating such traditionally male jobs as laborers more than such women's jobs as inspectors? Moreover they argue that the selection of compensable factors in a job evaluation system tends to discount the content and importance of women's jobs and to overvalue the same factors in men's jobs.

To remedy the perceived problem, the EEOC is considering reliance on the *Griggs v. Duke Power Company*[2] disparate impact test as the vehicle with which to press comparable worth claims. Thus, a prima facie case would be established if a company utilizes a neutral compensation system, such as a job evaluation plan, that results in predominantly female jobs receiving lower wages than predominantly male jobs.[3] Once the prima facie violation is established, the burden would shift to the employer to show that the job evaluation system is job-related or justified by business necessity—an extremely difficult task under Title VII case law.

Fallacies in the Comparable Worth Theory

Both the sociological and legal underpinnings of the comparable worth theory, when closely examined, blow away like a wisp of smoke.

Sociological Forces

Proponents of the comparable worth theory contend that jobs predominantly held by women are undervalued solely because women hold them. They argue that if traditionally female jobs had been historically filled on a sex-blind basis, the jobs would pay higher wages and salaries. It is this premise that provides the foundation of the comparable worth theory. On the other side of the coin, however, the sociological evidence is highly persuasive that until recently, because of their lack of skills and discontinuous participation in the work force, and by their own decision, women have held the least responsible, demanding, and skilled jobs—and, consequently, the lowest paying jobs in the marketplace. Contrary to the position of

179

comparable worth theorists, it is not that female work is undervalued but rather that females have held jobs that would have a low value in the marketplace, regardless of the sex of the occupant.

Until recently, traditional sex role differentiation assigned women primary responsibility for child rearing and household duties, while the man in the family was the bread winner. These sex roles began at birth and affected choice of occupation, location and hours of work, education and length of time in the work force. This age-old division of household and familial obligations has resulted in women choosing traditionally female occupations (i.e., nurses, teachers, secretaries, and nonphysical factory jobs). Moreover, this role differentiation also has a significant impact on the extent of a woman's participation in the labor force.

Because of their traditional childbearing and child rearing responsibilities, women's participation in the labor force is erratic. In fact, one authority has determined that working women on the average are out of the labor force for over ten years during their working life.[4] According to the "theory of human capital," the distribution of earnings within the labor sector is determined by the workers' human capital. Individuals, through their own choice, can determine the value of their human capital by adding to their level of education, experience and time in the job market, and choice of career path. Women, until recently, have opted for discontinuous participation in the work force, less demanding career paths, and work in a limited category of jobs that permitted easier entry into and out of the labor market to allow for childbearing and to fulfill family needs.[5] Hence, it would appear that the male-female wage disparity results not so much from undervalued women's jobs but rather from the women themselves who either opt for or are limited to jobs carrying the least economic value in our society.

The decided preference held by women for certain kinds of work cannot be overemphasized as a factor precipitating the male-female wage disparity. A recent study conducted for the U.S. Department of Labor concluded that women frequently entered low-paying occupations solely as a result of their own preference. Noting a decisive preference of both college educated and blue collar women for occupations typically held by women, the study observed that proponents of affirmative action programs are flatly wrong in their contention that the preference of employers for women in certain occupations is responsible for occupational segregation. The vast majority of working

180

women not only have opted for typically female jobs but also state that their aspirations for the future are for traditionally female jobs.[6]

In response to these points, comparable pay advocates point to pay differentials between traditionally male and female jobs requiring comparable education and training. For what reason other than sex discrimination, they ask, do elementary school teachers, a predominantly female occupation, earn less than male business executives in light of comparable education and training? This argument is based on the assumption that occupations similar in their demands for knowledge and responsibility will pay equal wages in the absence of discrimination. According to a recent study, "this assumption is incorrect. Occupations [similar] in all such characteristics still exhibit considerable variations in earnings. Econometric studies [demonstrate that] experience and education typically explain only about ⅓ of the variation in earnings, *even when the sample is restricted to white males*."[7]

A rather obvious conclusion arises from these phenomena. While some female occupational segregation is due to past intentional sex discrimination, the main reasons result from factors such as female disinclination, intermittent female participation in the labor force, and lesser skills and education of female workers—matters over which corporations bear no present legal responsibility. Since, until recently, women came to the labor market with less to offer in terms of human capital and, in most cases, opted for jobs that were the least demanding and provide the most flexibility for entering and leaving the labor market, we must conclude that it is not that female jobs are undervalued but rather that females choose jobs of the least value. Hence, the appropriate remedy is not to raise wages but rather to break down occupational segregation.

Marketplace Forces

Comparable pay theorists contend that job evaluation plans contain a built-in bias that results in wholesale undervaluation of the female jobs in industry.

Job evaluation plans are used to determine the relative worth of jobs within a company. Most job evaluation plans in use today are "point systems" containing approximately ten factors measuring such job elements as mental skill, manual skill, physical effort, and hazards. Within each factor are various degrees—labelled, for example,

(A, B, C, D)—each affording a number of points. A typical plan might provide that if a particular job is rated at the B level for mental effort, it would receive three points; if rated at the C level, six points, and so on. The sex discrimination issue arises because job evaluation plans grant higher points for some factors than others, i.e., a degree rating of B under the "employment training and experience" factor affords more points than a B degree rating under the "mental skill" factor. In many, if not most cases, these differences in the weight of factors in job evaluation plans are directly or indirectly tied into the marketplace's determination of what the various job skills are worth.

Advocates of the comparable pay theory attack the conventional job evaluation plans, claiming that traditionally male factors, such as physical efforts, are given higher points or weights than traditionally female factors, such as mental effort and manual skill (dexterity). Criticisms of current job evaluation plans rest on two assumptions: first, the proposition that there is some objective determination of job worth apart from the marketplace and, second, that the marketplace's influences on job evaluation plans and wages result in an inaccurate and sex-influenced assessment of the job's worth.

The EEOC has recently commissioned a study by the National Academy of Sciences to determine whether job measurement procedures can be developed to objectively assess the worth of jobs. The academy's interim report highlights the dangers implicit in the government's foray into this area. While the academy concludes that some job evaluation plans may be biased by giving less weight to traditionally female factors than to male factors, it gives no indication of what objective determinates can be used to arrive at the "true worth" of jobs. Indeed, a definition of worth is never given.

The academy's reticence is understandable since any determination in a vacuum of factor or job worth involves the most subjective of judgments. Why should some job evaluation factors be worth more than others? While the physical effort factor (a traditionally male factor) is generally given substantial weight in job evaluation plans, so is the education factor—a sex-neutral factor. Is education overvalued as a compensable factor? On the other hand, why should high-rise contruction workers earn more than many college professors? Why is a good executive secretary worth more than many architects? The answer, of course, lies not with an esoteric, metaphysical analysis of factor weights but rather with the free market economy in which market forces and supply and demand determine the worth of the elements of jobs and ultimately fix the wages of workers, from quarterbacks to electricians to steelworkers. If the supply of workers exceeds the employer's demand, the employer will lower the wages for that job until the supply of workers equals the demand. A shortage of qualified accountants will cause their wages to rise, just as a glut of engineers once forced their wages down and an undersupply now forces their wages up.

Any viable job evaluation plan captures market factors by determining the weight of the various factors within the plan. Indeed, if there is any objective determinate of the worth of the job, it is the job's market wage rate. If an employer must pay more to obtain workers who perform physical labor than to get workers who use manual skill, the job evaluation plan will reflect those supply and demand considerations. In the final analysis, the worth or value of jobs is determined by those individuals best suited to make the determination—the employer and the employee—through the supply and demand interaction.

If comparable pay advocates have their way and the market is prevented from working because of the imposition of artificial factors, the results will be disastrous. The moment one admits that a job hierarchy exists, that a Fortune 500 chief executive officer should be paid more than a janitor, value judgments about job content must be made. Such value judgments reflect not only what elements of the job should be accorded weight in a job evaluation plan but also how much weight. In making such value judgments, no system is without bias. Our society, founded on the principle that the unfettered forces of supply and demand determine price, would be severely compromised if courts recognized a cause of action for comparable worth.

Problems in Establishing a
Comparable Worth Violation

Proponents of the comparable worth theory assert that a prima facie violation may be shown under the *Griggs v. Duke Power Company*[8] disparate impact theory. They contend that it is necessary simply to establish that an ostensibly neutral job evaluation system adversely affects female employees when that system results in the lowest ratings and, hence, the lowest wages to those jobs with a 70 percent or more female population.

This suggestion misconstrues the *Griggs* theory. As defined by the U.S. Supreme Court, *Griggs* prohibits "employment procedures or testing mechanisms that operate as 'built in head wind' for minority groups and are unrelated to measuring job capability." Simply stated, *Griggs* prohibits barriers to hiring or promotion that have an adverse effect on females or minorities. This was underscored by the Supreme Court in *Albemarle Paper Co. v. Moody*:

> "[A] *prima facie* case of discrimination— . . . [is] shown . . . [when the] test in question selects applicants for *hiring* or *promotion* in a racial pattern significantly different from that of the pool of applicants."[9] [Emphasis added.]

In 1978, in the *City of Los Angeles v. Manhart*, the Supreme Court addressed the suggestion that a gender-neutral pension plan would violate Title VII because of its disproportionately heavy impact on male employees. The Court stated that the male employees would not prevail in a Title VII action since "even a completely neutral practice will inevitably have some disproportionate impact on one group or another. *Griggs* does not imply, and this Court has never held, that discrimination must always be inferred from such consequences."[10]

That the Supreme Court intended the *Griggs* test to apply solely to job prerequisites is reinforced by the absence of viable case law involving the successful application of the disparate impact test to a claim of discriminatory compensation.

Application of the *Griggs* test to job evaluation systems suffers a second fatal flaw. In every case decided under the *Griggs* doctrine, the plaintiff has shown a direct adverse effect on individuals. *Griggs* was not intended to apply when the neutral criteria (i.e., a job evaluation plan) has an adverse effect on a series of jobs and only a consequential effect on the incumbents of the jobs. *Griggs* requires a *direct* adverse effect on individuals. Job evaluation plans, when applied, have an impact by assigning to the job a rating that ultimately determines the wage of the job. Any adverse effect on females or minorities as a result of an application of a job evaluation plan is secondary; and the *Griggs* theory does not render unlawful such secondary effect.

The sheer folly in applying the disparate impact test to job evaluation plans is shown in the following example. Suppose an airline used a job evaluation plan to rate airline pilots and stewardesses. The plan gave substantial weight to the factor of "responsibility for the safety of others," thus resulting in substantially higher ratings and hence salary for pilots than for stewardesses. Assuming that the position of pilot was predominantly male and that of stewardess predominantly female, the comparable pay interpretation of the *Griggs* theory would indicate a prima facie case of discrimination. Such a result would defy logic. Moreover, *Griggs* was not intended to put courts in the position of evaluating whether an airline was justified in giving an 80 percent weight to the safety factor as opposed to a 50 percent or 90 percent weight. This type of value judgment has nothing to do with sex discrimination.

Above all, there is no necessity for application of the disparate impact test even if a job evaluation plan does undervalue predominantly female jobs, since both the discrimination (if any) and the remedy are achieved in a far more direct manner. Sex-segregated job classifications standing alone constitute a prima facie case of discrimination, and Title VII mandates that courts eradicate barriers to promotion and award back pay to the affected class. Hence, any pay disparity suffered by female employees as a result of illegal sex-segregated job classifications is directly remedied through traditional Title VII judicial remedies.

Comparable pay advocates also assert that even in the absence of a neutral job evaluation system the mere existence of sex-segregated job classifications, where the jobs held predominantly by women pay lower wages than those held by men, constitutes a prima facie case of comparable pay discrimination. With this claim, they shift to the employer the burden to justify the reasons for the disparity. This theory, too, skims along on thin ice. The underpinning of a statistical inferential case rests on the premise that numbers alone can be used to draw an inference to establish a fact. Thus, when blatant statistical segregation occurs, courts will infer that women or blacks have been illegally excluded and shift the burden to the employer to explain why.[11]

The assertion by comparable pay proponents that the statistics showing segregated jobs establish a judicial inference that the jobs held predominantly by females are undervalued relative to jobs held by males stretches the sublime to the ridiculous. Indeed, under this theory if a company placed all of its male employees in skilled craft jobs and all the female employees in menial ditch-digging jobs, a judicial inference would be drawn that the ditch-digger job paid less than the skilled craft job solely because females held the position—hardly a logical inference. Less hypothetically, since most secretaries are women and most executives males, can it be inferred that the pay differential between the two groups is substantially related to the sex of the job-holders?

Thus, even if plaintiffs are permitted to litigate comparable pay claims, short of the rare "smoking gun" situation in which there is direct evidence that a company pays less for female-held jobs solely because they are held by females, plaintiffs face a difficult, if not impossible, task in establishing the existence of a violation.

The Absence of Statutory Authority

While the crusade on behalf of comparable pay is new, the concept of comparable pay is not. The possibility that civil rights advocates might use federal equal employment opportunity legislation to litigate comparable worth cases was considered and decisively rejected by Congress.

The original versions of the Equal Pay Act introduced in Congress in 1962 mandated equal pay for work of *comparable* character on jobs involving *comparable* skills.[12] After an extensive debate, the scope of the bill was scaled down from the broad "comparable work" standard to a standard requiring "equal work for jobs the performance of which required skill, effort and responsibility and which are performed under similar working conditions." The legislative history is replete with reflections of congressional intent to immunize wages set through the workings of the market, the bargaining process, or job evaluation systems. Moreover, the unambiguous legislative history shows that Congress did not intend to authorize the government or the courts to unilaterally determine wage rates by substituting their own concept of economic worth for that of employers.

Judicial application of the Equal Pay Act has been wholly in accordance with congressional intent, and the courts have required plaintiffs to prove that the disputed jobs are substantially equal in content and skill, effort and responsibility, and working conditions.[13]

In contrast to the extensive legislative history surrounding the promulgation of the Equal Pay Act, the history of the enactment of the sex discrimination prohibition of Title VII of the Civil Rights Act of 1964 is, as the Supreme Court has stated, "notable primarily for its brevity."[14]

The sex discrimination prohibitions were inserted into Title VII as a last-minute diversionary tactic by a group of southern congressmen who ultimately voted against passage of the entire Civil Rights Act.[15] On the basis of this history, it is incredible to assume that Congress intended, *sub silentio*, to create a cause of action for comparable worth claims that would reverse its decision, made one year earlier during the promulgation of the Equal Pay Act, to obviate such claims.

Once it became clear that sex discrimination would remain part of the proposed Title VII legislation, the Senate became acutely aware that the broad language of the Act might be vulnerable to interpretations that would undermine the efforts of Congress to construct the effective wage discrimination standard already embodied in the Equal Pay Act. To prevent this possibility, Senator Wallace F. Bennett of Utah proposed an amendment to insure that the Equal Pay Act's standard would apply to wage discrimination claims regardless of whether the claim was brought under the Equal Pay Act or Title VII.[16] Discussion of the meaning of the Bennett Amendment in both the House and Senate shows that Congress intended that if an employer complied with the Equal Pay Act, it likewise complied with Title VII.[17]

Advocates of the comparable pay theory argue that the Bennett Amendment was meant to incorporate only the four affirmative defenses of the Equal Pay Act.[18] Such an interpretation, however, would render the Bennett Amendment meaningless. The first three affirmative defenses had already been explicitly incorporated into Title VII in the very section in which the Bennett Amendment is found, section 703(h).[19] The fourth affirmative defense (i.e., payments based on "any other factor other than sex") is obviously fundamental to Title VII, which forbids employers to discriminate "because of sex."[20] Thus, if the sole purpose of the Bennett Amendment were to incorporate the four affirmative defenses into Title VII, it would have been redundant to repeat the defenses contained in the same section of the Act.[21]

Virtually every court confronted with the possible interaction of the Equal Pay Act and Title VII in wage discrimination matters has adopted the interpretation that Title VII is expressly limited by the parameters of the Equal Pay Act. In fact, this issue has been considered twenty-one times by various district courts and U.S. courts of appeals and, in all but two of those cases, the court has interpreted the equal pay for equal work standard limitation.[22]

Conclusion

There is, to say the least, a curious tension between the comparable worth theory and the equal opportunity laws. One of the important goals of the latter is to make available higher paying jobs to groups that have been arbitrarily excluded from such jobs. But, rather than alleviating occupational segregation, the comparable worth theorists would reinforce such occupational ghettos by paying women more money to stay in traditionally women's jobs. This approach would vitiate the economic incentive to move away from such work.

The notion of equality of results, rather than of opportunities, permeates the comparable worth theory. Moreover, a strong element of social engineering is inherent in the comparable worth theory that the value of a person's labor and skill can be calculated in a vacuum, outside the market. Refusing to recognize that people make conscious choices to be a nurse rather than a truck driver, to be a school teacher rather than a plumber, to be an inspector rather than a laborer, the comparable worth theorists want no cost to attach to such choices. Further, without the slightest concern about the drastic consequences to our economy, they want employers to foot the bill, even though the forces that lead to occupational segregation, such as the availability of labor and disinclination of women to hold certain jobs, occur outside the workplace. Whatever the root cause of the earnings gap between men and women, its solution lies not in comparable worth, the effects of which would amount to revolution, but in the existing legal structure.

NOTES

1. Lev. 27:3-4.

2. 401 U.S. 424 (1971).

3. A female job is one in which 70 percent to 80 percent of the work force is composed of women.

4. S. Polachek, "Discontinuous Labor Force Participation and Its Effect on Women's Market Earnings," *Sex Discrimination and the Division of Labor*, (Columbia University Press, 1975).

5. See, Sandell, "Economic Quality for Women," 62 *American Economic Review* 175 (May 1975), and Frank, "Why Women Earn Less: The Theory and Estimation Differential Overqualification," 68 *American Economic Review* (June 1978).

6. "A Longitudinal Study of the Educational and Labor Market Experience of Young Women," *Years For Decision*, Volume IV, U.S. Department of Labor Employment and Training Administration, (Washington, D.C.: Department of Labor, 1978). This study was conducted under a contract from the Department of Labor with the Center for Human Resource Research of the Ohio State University. The study involved a nationwide scientific survey

of approximately 5,000 noncollege and college females over a five-year period.

7. Cotton Mather Lindsay, "Equal Pay for Comparable Work: An Economic Analysis of a New Anti-Discrimination Doctrine," (University of Miami's Law and Economic Center, 1980).

8. 401 U.S. 424 (1971). *See* Blumrosen, "Wage Discrimination, Job Segregation, And Title VII of The Civil Rights Act of 1964," 12 *Journal of Law Reform*, (Spring 1979).

9. 22 U.S. 405 (1970).

10. 435 U.S. 702 (1978).

11. *Parham v. Southwestern Bell Telephone Co.*, 433 F.2d 421 (8th Cir. 1970); *Hazelwood School District v. United States*, 433 U.S. 299 (1977).

12. H.R. 8898, 87 Cong., 1st Sess.; H.R. 10226, 87 Cong., 2d Sess.

13. *Shultz v. Wheaton Glass Company*, 421 F.2d 259, 265 (3d Cir.), *cert. denied*, 398 U.S. 905 (1970); *Hodgson v. Brookhaven General Hospital*, 436 F.2d 719 (5th Cir. 1970); *Hodgson v. Miller Brewing Company*, 457 F.2d 221 (7th Cir. 1972); *Usery v. Allegheny County Institution District*, 544 F.2d 148 (3d Cir. 1976); *Horner v. Mary Institute*, No. 79-1352 (8th Cir., January 14, 1980).

14. *General Electric Company v. Gilbert*, 429 U.S. 125, 143 (1976).

15. *Legislative History of Title VII and IX of the Civil Rights Act of 1964*, pp. 3213-3215, 10 *Cong. Rec.* 2577-84, 2804-05 (1964).

16. The amendment provides in pertinent part:
It shall not be unlawful employment practice under this Title for any employer to differentiate upon the basis of sex in determining the amount of wages or compensation paid or to be paid to employees of such employer if such differentiation is authorized by the provisions of Section 6(d) of the Fair Labor Standards Act of 1938, as amended (29 U.S.C. 206(d)).

17. *Legislative History of Title VII*, 3031; 111 Cong. Rec. 13359.

18. The specific exemptions are:
Where such payment is made pursuant to (i) a seniority system; (ii) a merit system; (iii) a system which measures earnings by quantity or quality of production; or (iv) a differential based on any other factor other than sex. 29 U.S.C. § 206(d)(1).

19. Section 703(h) provides:
(h) Notwithstanding any other provisions of this Title, it shall not be an unlawful employment practice for an employer to apply different standards of compensation, or different terms, conditions, or privileges of employment pursuant to a bona fide seniority or merit system, or a system which measures earnings by quantity or quality of production. 42 U.S.C. § 2000e-2(h).

20. 42 U.S.C. § 2000e-2(a).

21. Only one court has adopted the comparable pay advocates' interpreta-

tion of the Bennett Amendment. *Gunther v. County of Washington,* 602 F.2d 882 (9th Cir. 1979).

22. The lead cases are: *Christensen v. State of Iowa,* 563 F.2d 353 (8th Cir. 1977); *Lemons v. City & County of Denver,* 17 FEP Cases 906 (D. Colo. 1978); *Orr v. Frank R. MacNeill & Son,* 511 F.2d 166 (5th Cir.), *cert. denied,* 423 U.S. 865 (1975); *Chrapliwy v. Uniroyal,* 15 FEP Cases 795 (N.D. Ind. 1977); *Angelo v. Bacharach Instrument Co.,* 555 F.2d 1164 (3d Cir. 1977); *IUE v. Westinghouse Electric Corp.,* 19 FEP Cases 450 (D.N.J. 1979). But see *Gunther v. County of Washington,* 602 F.2d 882 (9th Cir. 1979); *Fitzgerald v. Sirloin Stockade,* __ F.2d __, 22 FEP Cases 262 (10th Cir. 1980).

SEXUAL HARASSMENT

Sexual Harassment in the Workplace—
What Should the Employer Do?

Mary D. Faucher and Kenneth J. McCulloch

The "casting couch" on which aspiring actresses enhance their chances of becoming stars may soon become a thing of the past. Producers, instead of enjoying a "fringe benefit," may find themselves being sued for sex discrimination when they suggest that the road to stardom entails a detour into the bedroom. This is because several courts have recently determined that when a supervisor makes sexual advances and conditions a promotion or the retention of a job on the acceptance of these advances, he[1] may be liable for sex discrimination under Title VII.[2] Title VII makes it an unlawful employment practice

---

Ms. Faucher is an associate with the law firm of Townley & Updike, New York City. She is a June 1977 graduate of Yale Law School and a *magna cum laude* graduate of the Georgetown University School of Foreign Service.

Mr. McCulloch graduated from Fordam Law School in 1968. He is a partner in the firm of Townley & Updike, New York City, and was previously New York Regional Counsel for Equal Employment Opportunity Commission and an attorney, Equal Employment, Philadelphia Litigation Center.

for an employer to discriminate against any individual with respect to conditions or privileges of employment on the basis of sex.

Sexual harassment on the job may take several forms. When do these various forms of sexual harassment on the job constitute sex discrimination? A supervisor may condition a promotion on fulfillment of his sexual desire, he may simply make a sexual advance, or he may verbally harass the employee by making repeated references to physical characteristics of women or use phrases like "women are illogical." The courts that have addressed the problem of sexual harassment have faced only the issue of a superior's sexual advances acceptance of which was made the condition of a promotion or job retention. This discussion will examine those court decisions, but it will also include an analysis of other forms of sexual harassment and will offer employers faced with the problem of sexual harassment suggestions including preventing, investigating, and avoiding corporate liability for it.

Prefatory to analyzing the court decisions, it is necessary to understand problems facing the judiciary. On the one hand, courts have not desired to increase the EEOC's backlog by making every complimentary remark or flirtatious approach to a member of the opposite sex the basis for a cause of action under Title VII. On the other hand, in recent decisions the courts are increasingly recognizing that there is a point beyond which a person in a supervisory position should not be permitted to abuse his power by making a sexual demand on an employee. Thus far, in all cases that have been the subject of judicial opinion, a supervisor-subordinate relationship was involved, there was present the potential for retaliation by the supervisor whose approaches were rejected, and actual retaliatory action by such supervisor was alleged to have occurred. Apparently, as the law now stands, employees who make sexual advances to a co-worker, and thus are not in a position to retaliate should their advances be rejected, are in a much better position to continue such advances immune to the strictures of Title VII. However, for such employees we anticipate that there will develop a body of law equating their conduct to situations in which co-workers use racial epithets or make derogatory ethnic or racial remarks. In such situations, once the employer is put on notice of such conduct and is apprised of the fact that such remarks are objectionable, there arises the legal requirement for the employer to prevent such conduct. While this is not the state of the law at present, we anticipate that it will be, and that employers should administer their personnel policies now to protect themselves from liability for such conduct.

The courts initially determined that sexual propositions made by a supervisor do not give rise to a cause of action under Title VII. In *Corne v. Bausch & Lomb, Inc.*, 390 F. Supp. 161, 10 FEP Cases 289 (D. Ariz. 1975), *vacated and remanded on other grounds*, 562 F.2d 55, 15 FEP Cases 1370 (9th Cir. 1977), the plaintiffs alleged that their supervisor's sexual advances made working conditions so onerous that they were forced to resign from their jobs. The court held that there was no cause of action under Title VII against either the supervisor or the employer, because the supervisor was satisfying a personal urge and there was no employer policy involved. The employer had no responsibility for the "verbal and physical advances of the supervisor" because these advances had no relationship to the nature of employment.[3]

In all cases following *Corne*, however, the courts have determined that the employee does have a cause of action under Title VII where the supervisor conditions career enhancement on sexual submission *and* an employer policy or employer acquiescence is involved. What constitutes an employer practice or employer acquiescence has been the central issue with which the courts have wrestled in addressing the sexual advances problem.

In *Williams v. Saxbe*, 413 F. Supp. 654, 12 FEP Cases 1092 (D.D.C. 1976), *appeal pending*, the court made a distinction between a pattern or practice of imposing a condition of sexual submission on female employees and a non-employment-related personal encounter. The court went on to state that any policy or practice of a supervisor was automatically a policy or practice of the employer. In *Miller v. Bank of America*, 418 F. Supp. 233, 13 FEP Cases 439 (N.D. Cal. 1976), *appeal pending*, the court held that the employer was not liable for the supervisor's actions because the employer had a stated policy against such conduct, the employer had a formal department to which an employee could complain about such conduct, and the plaintiff had never complained to that department. In *Barnes v. Costle*, _____ F.2d _____, 15 FEP Cases 345 (D.C. Cir. 1977), the court stated that an employer generally is chargeable for discriminatory practices of a supervisor, but where the supervisor contravenes employer policy without the employer's knowledge, and the employer rectifies the consequences when the conduct is discovered, the employer may be relieved from liability. In *Tomkins v. Public Service Electric & Gas Co.*, _____ F.2d _____, 16 FEP Cases 22 (3d Cir. 1977), the court determined that where an employer has actual or constructive knowledge of a supervisor's conduct and does not take prompt and appropriate remedial action, Title VII is violated. The Fourth Circuit agreed with that approach. *Garber v. Saxon Business Products*, _____ F.2d _____, 15 FEP Cases 344 (4th Cir. 1977).

The cases demonstrate that the plaintiff must show that the sexual advances of the supervisor were a condition of employment and were not personal, non-employment-related encounters. In all cases other than *Corne*, the plaintiffs eventually were terminated after refusing their supervisors' propositions. All courts other than the *Corne* court required actual or constructive knowledge by the employer of the supervisor's conduct, through either a direct complaint, knowledge of other supervisory personnel, or acquiescence in the termination. The courts have determined that it is not necessarily sexual advances that violate Title VII, but the retaliatory measures taken once these advances are refused, that make the conduct a condition of employment that violates Title VII.

While the law is relatively clear regarding a direct sexual proposition by a supervisor, it is less clear regarding the remarks that usually precede the direct proposition. In *Tomkins*, the plaintiff also suggested to the court that Title VII mandates that employees be afforded "a work environment free from the psychological harm flowing from an atmosphere of discrimination." The plaintiff made an analogy to EEOC decisions where violations of Title VII were found when employees were subjected to racial and ethnic epithets. The court, in a footnote, determined that because it held that the facts as alleged constituted a sex-based condition of employment, it did not need to reach this alternative theory.

Other forms of sexual harassment, such as referring to women as "girls," maintaining that "women are dumb" or that they "can't take pressure," or remarking on physical characteristics, can be analogized to situations in a racial or ethnic context where employees refer to co-workers in derogatory terms. Although one court has recently determined that the use of derogatory comments must be "excessive and opprobrious" to become discriminatory, *Caradidi v. Kansas City Chiefs Football Club, Inc.*, _____ F.2d _____, 15 EPD ¶ 8014 (8th Cir. 1977), most courts have generally held that such conduct does constitute racial or ethnic harassment, but that where the employer makes a diligent effort to eliminate such conduct, it is not responsible. Where the employer is on notice of the existence of such conduct, it must at least take some positive action to avoid liability. Moreover, one court has determined that where a supervisor, in his supervisory capacity, has knowledge of the conduct, this constitutes knowledge to the employer, *Anderson v. Methodist Evangelical Hospital*, 4 FEP Cases (W.D. Ky. 1971), *aff'd*, 4 FEP Cases 987 (6th Cir. 1972), and another court has adopted the rationale that an employer is presumed responsible for any actions of its supervisory personnel. *Ostapowicz v. Johnson Bronze Co.*, 369 F. Supp. 522, 7 EPD ¶ 9211 (W.D. Pa. 1973), *aff'd in part, rev'd in part*, 541 F.2d 394 (3d Cir. 1976).

The EEOC, in making reasonable-cause determinations, has been more liberal in imposing employer liability where supervisors use racial or ethnic epithets or employ religious intimidation. For example, where a supervisor constantly preached to employees, the EEOC found reasonable cause and maintained that the employer was responsible for actions of its supervisors and that the employee had no obligation to inform higher-level management of the intimidation. The EEOC has also maintained that, at the very least, positive action is required where such action is necessary to redress the harassment, and that where such positive action is taken the supervisor's conduct will not be imputed to the employer. Generally, according to the EEOC, an employer is obliged to maintain a working environment free of racial intimidation or insult.

Repeated references to women in a derogatory manner ("girls," "women are dumb") would appear to constitute a Title VII violation where the employer takes no action, as in the racial-epithet context mentioned above. The EEOC has determined that constant referral to women as "girls" is sufficient for a reasonable-cause determination that Title VII has been violated. EEOC Decision No. 72-0679, 1973 CCH EEOC Decisions, ¶ 6324 (Dec. 27, 1971). However, no court has discussed the applicability of this analogy, and courts would probably be reluctant to apply it. In the sexual-advances cases, courts have demonstrated their reluctance to address the issue of verbal harassment because "flirtations of the smallest order would give rise to liability." *Miller, supra*, at 441.

Nonetheless, in the racial-epithet context, the cases and EEOC determinations demonstrate that an employer is under a duty to investigate and eradicate such intimidation where it knows or should know that such conduct is occurring. Thus sexual harassment in the form of verbal abuse or sexual propositions could require the same employer action. In any event, recent case law addressing the problem of sexual harassment in the form of sexual advances as a condition of employment does imply that positive action on the part of the employer is required to avoid liability.

197

What constitutes positive action is not clear. The racial-epithet cases have held that a diligent investigation of complaints by the employer is sufficient. Certainly, the employer must do something. In *Miller*, the employer maintained a policy of preventing and prohibiting moral misconduct, including sexual advances, and calling for suspension, dismissal, and/or reprimand where this policy was contravened. The company also had an employee relations department to which complaints could be made and through which investigations were conducted. The court appeared to approve of this system, and because the employee alleging the advances did not take advantage of it, the court dismissed her complaint.

Moreover, the concurring opinion in *Barnes* suggests preventive measures by which the employer can avoid derivative liability: (1) post its policy against sexual harassment, (2) provide a workable mechanism for the prompt reporting of complaints, (3) include within this mechanism a rapid warning for the supervisor involved, and (4) afford the opportunity for the complainant to remain anonymous.

All the foregoing suggests that the intelligent employer should set up some kind of mechanism to handle complaints of sexual harassment. This need not be a separate apparatus, but could be made part of a department addressed to complaints of discrimination generally. Most companies already have at least informal procedures for processing complaints of employee mistreatment, but the development of a formal system appears warranted, in the discrimination area in general and in the area of sexual harassment in particular. Sometimes a sexual advance may not be offensive, and sexual liaisons between employees may not necessarily originate in the workplace. Nevertheless, complaints may arise from such situations, and a formal mechanism for handling such complaints will serve to weed out unfounded charges.

The investigatory and remedial action of an employer also raises problems that warrant a formalized procedure. Apart from the investigation, what form should the reprimand take—a warning, a note in the personnel file, or something else? If, after the investigation, the charges appear supported, the warning might be coupled with a determination that a second charge would mandate immediate suspension or dismissal. Alternatively, a demotion might be in order. The cases and EEOC decisions emphasize that a diligent investigation is required, but what if the investigation fails to reveal anything? This situation is very likely to arise where the case boils down to the word of the employee against the word of the supervisor. Where the investigation shows no foundation for the charge, other than the complaint itself, should the supervisor still receive a reprimand in some form? Obviously, some standard procedures should be set up to afford consistency and to demonstrate diligence on the part of the employer, but if an investigation cannot confirm the allegation, no reference to the allegation should be included in the personnel file of the accused employee, and no dissemination of the accusation should take place.

It should be reiterated that the cases involving sexual harassment have alleged a sexual advance by a supervisor to a subordinate and retaliatory action by the supervisor for refusal. This is a separate problem from the situation where an advance is made by one employee to another. In that situation it is unclear whether a sexual advance, in and of itself, constitutes sex discrimination. Courts have maintained that it is not the sexual advance, but the retaliatory action, that constitutes sex discrimination. However, in the case of advances by employees, an analogy can be made to those cases where co-workers used racial epithets or derogatory ethnic remarks. The authors feel that the courts eventually will apply such an analogy to sexual harassment by co-workers, and thus it would be wise to include in the investigatory mechanism the opportunity to complain of sexual advances alone. This would allow complaints to be made before damaging retaliatory action could be taken. Also, where co-workers are involved, it would allow the employer to put an end to the offensive conduct. As an example of such a comprehensive policy, the company in *Miller* prohibited sexual advances between *any* employees, not just between supervisors and employees working under them.

Obviously, problems peculiar to the individual fact situation may arise that require tailor-made remedies short of suspension or dismissal, such as transfer, warning, or some other kind of reprimand. Formal procedures, however, will help to create a fair system for addressing the problem and allow for reasonable resolution of complaints. What should be emphasized is that some mechanism should be developed, because sexual harassment, at least in the form of sexual advances by supervisors and retaliatory action for refusal, is a violation of Title VII, and therefore an employer is under an obligation to attempt to prevent it and to remedy it if it occurs.

There follow a sample notice that incorporates the philosophy of the courts in this legal area, and a flow chart that delineates the manner in which, at least for the present, employers might react to problems in this area.

CHART

Possible Procedure for Processing Complaints:

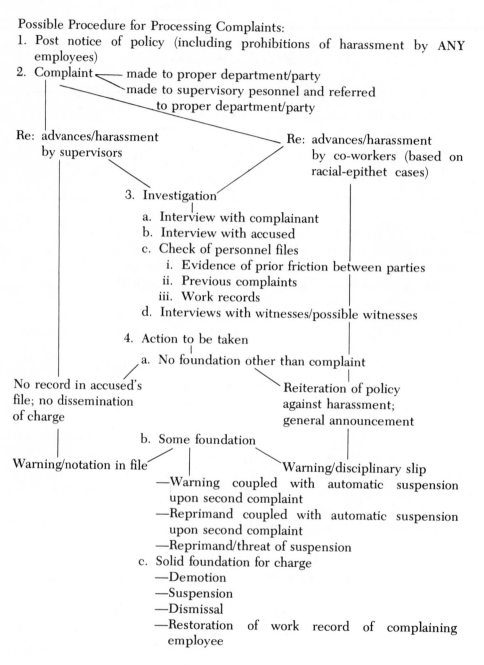

1. Post notice of policy (including prohibitions of harassment by ANY employees)

2. Complaint —— made to proper department/party
made to supervisory pesonnel and referred
to proper department/party

Re: advances/harassment
by supervisors

Re: advances/harassment
by co-workers (based on
racial-epithet cases)

3. Investigation
    a. Interview with complainant
    b. Interview with accused
    c. Check of personnel files
       i. Evidence of prior friction between parties
      ii. Previous complaints
     iii. Work records
    d. Interviews with witnesses/possible witnesses

4. Action to be taken
    a. No foundation other than complaint

No record in accused's
file; no dissemination
of charge

Reiteration of policy
against harassment;
general announcement

    b. Some foundation

Warning/notation in file

Warning/disciplinary slip

      —Warning coupled with automatic suspension upon second complaint
      —Reprimand coupled with automatic suspension upon second complaint
      —Reprimand/threat of suspension
    c. Solid foundation for charge
      —Demotion
      —Suspension
      —Dismissal
      —Restoration of work record of complaining employee

POSTER

OUR COURTS HAVE DECIDED
THAT RACIAL, ETHNIC, RELIGIOUS, OR SEXUAL
HARASSMENT ON THE JOB IS AGAINST THE LAW.
THIS COMPANY PROHIBITS VERBAL AND PHYSICAL
HARASSMENT OF ITS EMPLOYEES
BASED ON RACE, NATIONAL ORIGIN, RELIGION, OR SEX.

---

*Any employee subjected to such harassment
should file a complaint with the Supervisor of Personnel.*

NOTES

1. The male pronoun is used simply for convenience. This discussion is equally applicable to the case where a female supervisor makes sexual advances to a male employee.

2. Title VII of the Civil Rights Act of 1964, *as amended*, 42 U.S.C. §§ 2000e *et seq.*

3. The authors believe that the *Corne* decision will be reversed when the Ninth Circuit reviews the case on the merits. The case was remanded to the District Court to correct a jurisdictional defect in the plaintiff's case, and the Ninth Circuit would not have done this had it intended to affirm. See *Crosslin v. Mountain States Tel. & Tel. Co.*, 4 EPD ¶ 7577 (D. Ariz. 1971).

Sexual Harassment: New Guidelines, New Cases, New Problems

C. Daniel Karnes

Sexual harassment is moving out of the work place and into the courts.

There are eleven federal courts of appeals, each with its geographic jurisdiction of several states. Of the five that have been asked so far, all have held that sexual harassment is a form of sex discrimination that is actionable under Title VII.[1] At this time there is no reason to doubt that the remaining six circuits will follow the trend.

The Guidelines

The federal government also is paying closer attention to the issue. The two federal agencies responsible for the government's equal employment effort recently have issued guidelines dealing with the subject. The Office of Federal Contract Compliance Programs (OFCCP) has proposed to amend its sex-discrimination guidelines to prohibit sexual harassment among the work force of government contractors subject to Executive Order No. 11246. The OFCCP rules, which likely will become effective this summer, make it a violation of the Executive Order for an "official or supervisor" with any personnel au-

Mr. Karnes is with the Washington, D.C., office of Seyfarth, Shaw, Fairweather & Geraldson, specializing in equal employment litigation and federal contract compliance law. He was a supervisory trial attorney with the Equal Employment Opportunity Commission in Washington, D.C.

thority to take any action (favorable or unfavorable) based upon sexual advances, sexual favors, or a request for such favors, regardless of whether the affected employee acquiesces.[2] The OFCCP language is fairly straightforward. It prohibits sexual advances and requests for sexual favors when the objectionable action is taken by a person who can have some impact upon the affected employee's employment status. The OFCCP guidelines also make it a violation for a contractor to fail to take "appropriate corrective action" after becoming aware (or neglecting to take reasonable steps to become aware) of a violation.

The Equal Employment Opportunity Commission (EEOC) also has issued guidelines on the subject.[3] Characterized as "interim" guidelines, the EEOC rules went into effect upon their publication in the Federal Register, April 11, 1980, even though they are subject to public comment for sixty days and will be reissued in current or modified form sometime this summer. The fact that the EEOC issued "interim" guidelines reflects the importance the agency attaches to the subject.

The EEOC rules do not contain any earthshaking provisions. However, they do attempt to codify certain principles of employment discrimination law for application to cases of sexual harassment. The EEOC rules, however, are somewhat more detailed than those issued by the OFCCP. For example, the EEOC defines sexual harassment as "unwelcome sexual advances, requests for sexual favors, and other verbal or physical conduct of a sexual nature." Such conduct becomes actionable when it affects an individual's employment status ("terms and conditions of employment") adversely.

One section of the guidelines that is likely to cause concern to employers is the inclusion of conduct that creates "an intimidating, hostile, or offensive working environment." (Section 1604.11(a)(3).) This clause probably will be the most difficult for supervisors (and EEOC investigators) to interpret, because of its broadness and rather subjective standard.

The EEOC has indicated that it would "look at . . . the totality of the circumstances" when investigating such situations, but this is of little solace to the supervisor confronted with a complaint alleging an "offensive environment."

It also is not very comforting that the guidelines would confer absolute liability upon the employer for discriminatory acts of supervisors regardless of whether the employer knew of the supervisor's acts. The guidelines also impose liability for a nonsupervisory employee's conduct, if the employer knew of, or should have known of, the conduct. An employer is, however, allowed to avoid liability for nonsupervisory acts of sexual harassment if it can show that "immediate and appropriate corrective action" was taken when it became aware of such conduct.

The Cases

Although the courts have not yet had an opportunity to evaluate either agency's guidelines, some fairly clear patterns are beginning to emerge from the cases that have been decided to date.[4] In one of the leading sexual harassment opinions to be handed down by a federal appellate court, the U.S. Court of Appeals for the District of Columbia in *Barnes v. Costle* held that if a female employee's job "was abolished because she repulsed her male supervisor's sexual advances," she had a right under Title VII to pursue in the courts her claim of sex discrimination.[5] Although the court did not reach the merits of the plaintiff's claim, which was returned to the district court for trial, it issued a rather lengthy opinion discussing the legislative history of Title VII and the development of sex-discrimination case law.

(In an apparent tongue-in-cheek footnote that has been widely quoted, the court held that it also would be discriminatory for a homosexual supervisor to seek sexual favors from an employee of the same sex, but that a bisexual supervisor who approached employees of both sexes would escape liability as "the insistence upon sexual favors . . . would apply to male and female employees alike." (561 F.2d at 990 n. 55.).)

The courts, while confirming that sexual harassment is a litigable issue under Title VII, have imposed certain conditions on such claims. First, the conduct must have some direct employment consequences. It must in some definable way be related to a personnel action, such as a discharge, a promotion, a performance evaluation, or a training opportunity, or to a personnel inaction, such as a failure to hire, promote, or train. An example of the employment-consequences test is the decision of the First Circuit Court of Appeals in *Fisher v. Flynn* in which the court refused to credit the plaintiff's complaint of sexual harassment, as the plaintiff failed to allege a "sufficient nexus between her refusal to accede to the romantic overtures and her termination. She has not alleged that the department chairman had the authority to terminate her employment or effectively recommend the same. . . ."[6]

Second, most courts have required the plaintiff to show that the employer had actual or constructive knowledge of the allegedly unlawful conduct and failed to take action to correct the problem. That is, usually an employer will be held liable for the acts of a supervisor. If, however, it belatedly becomes aware of such acts, it may avoid liability if it takes prompt action to eliminate the problem.

Such corrective action might include warning or disciplining the supervisor, confirming to the complainant that positive steps have been taken to prevent a recurrence, and issuing a corporate policy on sexual harassment in general.

With regard to the issue of "constructive notice" to the employer, at least one court has held that a complaint to the supervisor who is the perpetrator of the unlawful conduct is not sufficient notice to the employer to create liability. *Vinson v. Taylor*, 22 Empl. Prac. Dec. ¶ 30,708 (D.D.C. 1980). An important factor in the court's decision in *Vinson* was that the employer had implemented and disseminated a corporate policy on sexual harassment.

The only decision, thus far, to impose liability upon individual co-workers for sexual harassment is *Kyriazi v. Western Electric*, in which the district court ordered three of the complainant's co-employees to pay $1,500 each in damages, and specifically forbade the employer from reimbursing the employees.[7] There is considerable doubt that this section of the ruling will be upheld on appeal. However, it is possible, especially in view of the EEOC guidelines, that the employer might be held liable for any damages caused by co-workers, if it can be shown that the employer failed to correct the problem once it became apparent.

Other federal district courts have declined, up to now, to follow the *Kyriazi* position. For example, in *Smith v. Rust Engineering Co.* the court dismissed a sexual harassment complaint against a co-employee because the defendant had no power to affect the plaintiff's "terms or conditions" of employment.[8] (Under the EEOC guidelines, the *employer* perhaps would have been liable for failing to maintain a working environment free of "intimidation.")

Suggestions

What can employers do to avoid problems of sexual harassment?

First, a specific policy statement on the subject should be prepared and circulated to all employees. The statement should explain what "sexual harassment" means in unmistakable terms, giving examples of prohibited conduct. It should indicate that discipline will be invoked for such misconduct. It should outline a specific complaint procedure for persons who feel they have been sexually harassed. This procedure should identify someone to contact if employees have questions on the subject.

Second, the employer should make certain that all supervisors understand the significance of this subject and the importance the employer attaches to it.

Third, if complaints arise, they should be investigated immediately with detailed records of all interviews, counseling, etc. It is especially important that the complaining party be informed of any action taken on the problem or the reasons such action may be inappropriate.

Conclusion

Sexual harassment cases currently are receiving a great deal of attention from the government compliance agencies and the courts. Employers should attempt to avoid problems in this area by utilizing a corporate policy and standard investigative procedure. If handled correctly, such a system need not interfere with the daily give-and-take of normal employee interaction, but will be available to deal with real problems as they arise.

NOTES

1. *Fisher v. Flynn*, 598 F.2d 663 (1st Cir. 1979); *Tomplin Tompkins v. Public Service Electric & Gas Co.*, 568 F.2d 1044 (3rd Cir. 1977); *Garber v. Saxon Business Products*, 552 F.2d 1032 (4th Cir. 1977); *Miller v. Bank of America*, 600 F.2d 211 (9th Cir. 1979); *Barnes v. Costle*, 561 F.2d 983 (D.C. Cir. 1977).

2. 41 C.F.R. § 60-20.8, published for comment at 44 Fed. Reg. 77006, 77017 (December 28, 1979).

3. 29 C.F.R. § 1604.11, published for comment at 45 Fed. Reg. 25024 (April 11, 1980).

4. Official agency guidelines, while they may be given great weight by courts, are not controlling and do not have the force of law, as formal regulations would. Thus, these guidelines should be viewed as the agencies' interpretation of Title VII and Executive Order No. 11246, not as rules of law.

5. *Barnes v. Costle*, 561 F.2d 983 (D.C. Cir. 1977).

6. 598 F.2d at 665.

7. 476 F. Supp. 335 (D.N.J. 1979).

8. 20 Fair Empl. Prac. Cas. 1172 (N.D. Ala. 1978).

CASE STUDIES

Women on the Line at Polaroid

Stanley M. Ginsberg

Until recently, women have fulfilled two kinds of roles in manufacturing companies: secretaries, or assembly-line labor. If there were any women at all in the ranks of management, they tended to be found in low-echelon, white-collar positions such as office manager, administrative assistant, and senior clerk.

With the appearance of recent EEO legislation, such as Revised Order No. 4, the transition of women from rank-and-file status to management remained confined, at first, to traditional white-collar areas of employment. Built-in biases—among both male production managers and women themselves—worked against the movement of women into the ranks of white-coated, clipboard-toting production line managers.

At light manufacturing companies—especially Fortune 500 companies like Polaroid Corp.—production management experience is the key to continued upward mobility for young executives. The reason is simple and straightforward: Line management tests a person's ability to deal with others and meet production goals. It also creates the kind of intimacy with the company's product and production methods that is virtually indispensable to successful middle and upper management. Thus, to exclude women from production supervision is to deprive them of the chance to reach significant positions of authority within the company.

Stanley M. Ginsberg, a New York City-based writer who covers business and management issues, also edits a monthly newsletter, *The Effective Manager*.

During late 1971 and early 1972, in response to requests from women's groups inside the company, Polaroid management set up three task forces charged with looking into the representation and utilization of women in the Polaroid work force. The results were sobering. Despite female representation through the total work force of 35 to 40 percent, women made up less than 1 percent of the line management staff of over 200. Even within the nonexempt work force, female employees were not distributed evenly among the various departments but tended to be ghettoized into manufacturing areas where the opportunies for upward movement were most limited.

At roughly the same time that the government issued Revised Order No. 4, Polaroid broadened its affirmative action planning to include women; development of AA goals and timetables for women had become a Polaroid priority even before the government got around to requiring them from contractors. Polaroid management established two goals: First, efforts had to be made to redistribute female workers among the manufacturing departments so that they were more or less at parity throughout the company; second, more women had to be brought into management positions.

Polaroid's solution was to look for qualified people within the company and provide greater opportunities for upward job mobility. Through an open posting system, a great many clerical and manufacturing workers crossed over into exempt positions. Since Polaroid is a firm believer in growing its own, the posting system continues to be a main source of qualified personnel. Also, women are now interviewed by campus recruiters for the same jobs that traditionally had been restricted to males only. Women now constitute 15 to 20 percent of total line management.

Despite Polaroid's initial efforts at opening management ranks to women, it took longer for significant numbers of women to appear in the ranks of production, materials management, and quality control supervisors than in traditional white-collar areas. Thus female movement was initially most visible in areas that customarily attracted women employees: personnel, finance, marketing, and the technical areas. This reflected several problems inherent in sexual stereotyping. One is that women are generally assumed to be either uninterested in or unsuited for the dirty, noisy machinery of the manufacturing divisions. A second factor—which really grows out of the first—is that women have traditionally been perceived as powerless, not only by men ("I don't take orders from women"), but also by other women, who have been socialized into acceptance of implicit male authority.

Polaroid has attempted to deal with the question of credibility and acceptance of female managers by developing "support groups" as part of its seminar program for new managers. In these groups, problems of managerial decision making, employee relations, and alternative ways of solving day-to-day management problems are discussed, with input from more experienced people. The groups also serve as a powerful means of instilling and maintaining the confidence of new managers by providing peer support. While these groups are beneficial to all employees, they are especially so for women supervisors, who must earn their spurs almost from the first instant on the job.

Thus far, Polaroid appears to be very successful. And as more and more women join supervisory ranks, worker acceptance of women supervisors continues to grow.

Perhaps the most exciting thing about Polaroid's approach to affirmative action for women is the complete openness of the system: As a matter of policy, the company strives to allow its employees to find their own level and encourages them to take jobs in the areas they are most interested in, even if those are not the jobs originally applied for. In one case, for example, a woman came to Polaroid from another company with a degree in counseling and a background in labor relations, but was hired as a quality control supervisor. After some time on the job she discovered a long-hidden interest in technology and, with a number of company-financed courses under her belt, has since moved on to a highly technical area. Another woman, with a degree in early childhood education, had been a secretary for several years, but was able to apply her classroom management skills to a supervisory position at which she is doing extremely well.

A few young managers are the "movers"; their interest and motivation take them to every corner of the company. One such person used her chemistry background to work as an assistant scientist in one of Polaroid's research divisions. After taking adult education courses in labor relations, she took a lateral move into the personnel area, where she worked for a year as a benefits administrator. Following a year's leave of absence, during which she returned to school for her M.B.A., she moved into the finance area as an auditor in domestic and international operations. At present, she is attached to the marketing area and manages a factory camera repair facility in Massachusetts. There is little doubt in anyone's mind that she will go very far in the company.

At present, the most important issue for Polaroid and most other companies in similar positions is the question of women's continuing movement into higher management echelons. For most male supervisors, two to four years of tenure represents the point at which they can expect promotion to the next highest rank—general supervisor, which is the first rung on the middle management ladder. Now that female supervisors have been on the job for the critical period, Polaroid's middle managers are beginning to find themselves with women in their own ranks, not just in managerial levels one or two steps further down the line.

The choice for middle management is not whether or not to bring women along—existing EEO statutes already have made that decision—but how to handle it. Employees are highly sensitive to their positions in the management structure, and any downgradings of their bosses' positions are inevitably perceived as corresponding prestige losses for themselves. This, in turn, could create enormous management problems not only for the hapless female manager, but for the corporation faced with a balky division as a whole.

Recent experience at Polaroid—principally in white-collar areas, where female managers tend to be two to three years ahead of production areas—has shown that women are moving into middle management, but that their representation at the general supervisor level is approximately 50 percent of their representation at the supervisor level. It is still too early to tell whether this is a function of the greater scrutiny given all candidates for middle management positions or whether it is the result of continuing discrimination.

As much as large corporations may be tempted to deny the existence of discrimination within management ranks, it does exist. Eli Ginzberg, professor at Columbia University's School of Business and chairman of the National Commission on Manpower Policy, has pointed out that "not everyone has gotten over the idea that women are not supposed to be bosses." He noted that in a society where men are educated to assume positions of dominance over women in both the home and the workplace a female boss "makes for just one additional problem in what is already a complicated relationship." Indeed, one respected executive recruiter admitted that many firms still refuse to consider female candidates for jobs in the $30,000-a-year category. "Clients will grab up the young female M.B.A. without any hesitation," he says, "but the higher you go, the more concern there is over reporting problems."

Susan Ells, whose personnel responsibilities at Polaroid include planning and development of affirmative action programs for women, has described the situation in this way: "The real question here is whether management will allow women to take that next key step—where they go from high-level individual contributors to positions where they have to manage other managers, and where the amounts of money at stake take a tremendous jump. So far, they have been terrific about helping women get ahead. Let's see what happens next."

Let us all see what happens next.

Career Development Workshops at Aetna Life & Casualty

"Like the first warm spring day"

Gloria J. Gery

A fully developed program to effect permanent change in the area of equal opportunity must consider three primary sets of barriers to change to be fully effective. *Organizational barriers*, such as the company's policies, systems, communications, and benefits, must be overcome in order to allow individual change to occur. *Managerial barriers*, those within individual managers or groups of managers that are evidenced by their attitudes, values, expectations, and behaviors, must then be minimized to allow the hiring, training, development, and promotion of women and minorities. And finally, barriers within women and minorities themselves, the *Intrapersonal barriers*, must be systematically dealt with. These barriers are the most subtle and complex, and manifest themselves in the attitudes, values, expectations, behaviors, self-confidence, and educational or experiential deficits of women and minorities. These result from a lifetime of social and educational conditioning that neither encouraged them toward business as a place where they can develop nor readied them for positions of independence, power, responsibility, and/or prestige. These barriers, because of their intangible and frequently psychological nature, are often the most resistant to change.

Ms. Gery is Manager, Equal Opportunity Program Development, Aetna Life & Casualty, Hartford.

214

One serious failure in many EEO efforts is the fact that corporate management or equal opportunity officers do not consider the equal opportunity issue as one that can be managed as any other business problem. Change is a result of a process with distinct phases that must be achieved *prior to* implementation of other specific efforts or programs. A classic example of failure to consider the process in its entire sequence is the immediate implementation of various forms of career development efforts, in either counseling or formal workshop form, without having changed the support systems to which the newly enthused woman or minority can return. For example, if job openings are not posted, or if individual managers are not yet aware of corporate expectations that women and minorities must receive specific developmental efforts or exposures, the career development workshop participant is subject to increased frustrations, with a concurrent growth in cynicism about organizational commitment to equal opportunity. This outcome would be the opposite of what the company wanted.

Career Development Workshops

In their proper context, career development workshops can be extremely powerful support for substantive individual change. Group dynamics and interaction and trainer skills and experience can combine to create significantly improved participant self-image, more precise individual career plans (which are frequently lacking or unrealistic within women or minorities), and increased personal involvement in and feelings about the organization. Group efforts can in most cases achieve these results more efficiently than individual counseling can, if the organization is large enough to allow groups to form where the participants do not usually work together, and where it is economical to develop an in-house program. In its efforts to deal with problems that women and minorities bring to the work force and to provide them with some of the tools they need to take greater control over and responsibility for their personal career development, Aetna Life & Casualty developed two workshops, Career Development for Women and Career Development for Minorities (minority women may attend either). While these workshops have been under way for only eight months, over 300 individuals have participated, and preliminary assessments by both the participants and corporate management are that they have effectively met their objectives. Participants' longer-term behavioral changes are now being researched

215

by a questionnaire to both participants and their immediate supervisors to be completed eight months after participation.

Workshop Objectives

The workshop has four specific objectives:
1. To develop skills in self-assessment and goal setting and to develop personal career/work action plans.
2. To provide a structured opportunity to deal with problems that may be unique to being a woman or minority in business today, and to develop strategies to overcome those barriers.
3. To deal with personal issues that are critical to effective planning, including those that might relate to race or sex. The latter would include such things as home/work conflicts, social issues, maintaining one's identity in basically white and male structure, and succeeding without compromising personal values.
4. To develop a peer support group among participants.

All of these are interrelated and are essential to give the individual participant a better grasp of what exactly he or she wants from the organization and how to go about increasing the chances of achieving it. The underlying premise of the design is that one *can* influence one's personal situation at work, even in a large, geographically dispersed, complex organization. The workshop leaders work with the group to develop practical behavioral solutions to problems that people encounter in their day-to-day situation. Solutions like "work harder" or "improve my attitude" are unacceptable.

Another assumption underlying the design of the workshop is that individuals cannot assess work situations and goals without considering their entire *personal* situation: the expectations they have of themselves and the demands placed on them by others at home, by the community, by their physical needs, and by their personal needs for growth in nonwork areas. One reality that must be dealt with is that commitments and time demands must be managed and that work goals for personal relationships, spiritual and intellectual growth, leisure needs, etc. With these in mind, the workshop design essentially forces the participant to deal with self in the context of one's complete life. It might more appropriately be called a Life and Career Planning Workshop, but particular organizational values at Aetna make the career development emphasis more appropriate at the present time.

216

Our experience has been that participants are greatly relieved to find this "whole person" orientation in the program. Some have initial reservations that the program is designed to rev everyone up to want to be a vice-president, and that new stereotypes of what one should want to become are being imposed on them (i.e., replacing the subordinate role with the power role). They want very much the option to choose their own definition of success. It is critical that participants and workshop leaders mutually understand that success is a personal definition and that it is just as "O.K." to decide to stay in one's current position as it is "O.K." to aspire to a different or higher-level job.

Participant critiques of the workshop include the following kinds of comments:

> Being myself and expressing my fears was very meaningful to me. I came with a lot of problems and I know I'm leaving with them, but I can now relate to my problems and I really feel I can handle them. I never realized I have a choice. Now I know I do and there is a way to accomplish my goals.

. . . .

> I will make time to plan my goals, to learn what I can do and where I can do it, if I decide I want to. I am also much more excited about Aetna as a living, changing structure. I previously felt that I should be happy to handle my own job well and that the whole of the organization was unapproachable. Now I think becoming more involved with the corporation will be interesting and exciting.

. . . .

> I am going to take more initiative and be sure my supervisors are aware that I view this as a career and are aware of my progress and potential. I am going to get off my butt!

. . . .

> I now know who I am and I am going to be myself—not something I am not. I know I am not the only one with problems we discussed. I have ways to handle my problems now. This workshop has been like the first warm spring day. I feel new and fresh. This is the first positive thing Aetna has done to help me develop my career.

Workshop Design

The workshop is a highly structured three-day program where approximately twenty-five participants work individually and in teams on activities designed to support the program objectives. Prior to the session, participants complete several questionnaires on themselves and their personal objectives; thus they begin to orient themselves to the program. In addition, they read a number of articles that relate to the whole concept of career development and, in particular, to some specific aspects that apply to women and/or minorities. Exhibit A lists the agenda for the program.

At the outset, the leader's objectives are to get the group comfortable in a situation they are somewhat apprehensive about. This is accomplished by sharing with the total group the reasons behind the development of the program and exactly what is going to go on for the next three days. A summary of individual participant objectives is given; a discussion as to whether or not the program is likely to meet those objectives establishes mutually understood expectations. Prior to attending, participants have anonymously sent in their personal reservations, which range from a concern about confidentiality of what is said to not wanting to discuss private thoughts and feelings with a group of people who are unknown—and these reservations are discussed in detail. Other typical concerns are that the session will be theoretical and a waste of time, or that it might turn into a gripe session where people share horror stories about discrimination. Airing these concerns minimizes anxiety as the workshop leader treats each issue. The introduction also includes a highly structured personal introductory activity that is later used as a vehicle for participants to get to know one another and as a basis for a discussion on giving and getting feedback from other people.

Team formation is the next step. Individuals choose their own teammates, making certain they are not in a group with anyone they work with or know very well. An interesting point to note is that people have little basis for making an intelligent selection of people they wish to work with. The workshop leaders show how analogous this is to real-life situations, such as deciding whether or not to take a job or whether or not to marry someone: We must often make critical decisions with little information. Later in the workshop, if individuals are dissatisfied with their team selection or feel they are not getting what they need from their group, this comparison to real life is extended: Participants are not allowed to change teams, just as they would not jump to another job or marriage without attempting to make things work. People must be led to understand on a personal level that they have a responsibility to do all they can to get what they need out of a situation or relationship, and this team is a typical example: They must take control and not let others ignore their needs or decide what is right for them.

Most of the activities require that individuals think about the activities privately, write down their thoughts in a personal workbook, and then discuss their thoughts with their team to the extent that they wish. The process of writing down specifics is essential to the program because it forces people to be much clearer and more concrete about themselves and their desires than they would be if they were only to think about it. In addition, committing oneself to paper increases the commitment to the feeling or belief or goal: people think things through more thoroughly when they write them down than if they simply fantasize. This written record also provides something for participants to refer back to and reflect on after their completion of the workshop.

Exhibit B is a sample of the Trainer Instructions for the activity on identifying strengths and weaknesses. These instructions are illustrative of the type of task activity, the type of climate the trainer must set, and the type of response that might have to be managed by the instructor.

Participant Expectations

Participants often have unrealistic expectations about what such a workshop will accomplish, and it is important to deal specifically with these throughout the program. Frequently, people think that this program is designed to provide them with job information and knowledge of career paths and job qualification requirements within the company. Other people feel that they will know themselves and their priorities completely and will have a definite career path and action plan at the end of the program. Some people expect that the workshop leader will have clear and immutable answers to the problems they identify as barriers to success.

Of course, none of this is possible in three days—or in three weeks. Throughout the session, the workshop leader must weave understanding of the program's objectives of giving *skills* and *approaches to take* that will allow the participants to continually self-assess, problem-solve, and learn of opportunities.

One way of bringing unrealistic expectations into line is to deal openly with each issue. For example, regarding the question of job information, the workshop leader usually mentions that one program considered but not adopted by the company, was on career paths and job requirements. Such a program was not offered because such specifics as career paths and job qualifications can change overnight with the stroke of an organization pen. What is important is to learn how to continuously get information about what is going on when there is no system to provide it on an ongoing basis. That is the real world: No one is going to hand you anything on a silver platter. You've got to find out how to get it.

Who Should Be a Trainer?

A number of factors must be considered in deciding what kinds of people should serve as trainers in-house career development workshops. Primary consideration should be given to the personal characteristics and skills of the individuals being considered. The trainer must be able to relate quickly to a broad cross-section of people and establish immediate credibility and trust. To do this, of course, requires an above-average level of self-assessment and self-worth. It is also critical that the trainer feel comfortable in being very open about self: personal experiences and characteristics, conflicts, objectives, etc. This openness is necessary not only to outline examples in giving instructions for each of the workshop activities but also to expose participants to a complete form of the process that a successful person has gone through. The trainer is in part a role model to the participants, and an ability to disclose personal information is a part of this. It is also highly desirable for the person to have achieved a measure of success within the organization. The actual achievement of a position of significance lends credibility to the process and provides role models for groups that have few.

One technique we have found particularly effective is a team-training approach. Following a number of successful workshops, the trainer selected participants from previous workshops and sought their involvement in the program as cotrainers. The objective was to provide a balance of trainer personalities and approaches in each session, reducing the chance of participants defining how they should behave or think by simply absorbing the style of the trainer. Participants have the following kinds of comments about such an approach:

> The two-leader style should be continued. You both complemented each other.

. . . .

> Each workshop leader knew her own style and stuck to it. It goes to show that you can be effective in a number of ways.

In addition, the opportunity to learn the skills of workshop leadership and the visibility afforded to the cotrainers have provided a significant personal developmental opportunity for these individuals.

Problems that Are Identified and Solutions that Are Offered

Career advancement problems, common to all of us, are sometimes complicated by being a woman or minority. Experiential and educational deficits, overcoming stereotypes that managers or customers hold, and dealing with sexism or racism in its subtle forms—all must be dealt with if the workshop is to meet its objectives. Listed below are some of the problems identified by workshop participants. An average workshop produces a list of thirty-five to forty problems that participants would like to deal with. Of course, not all are resolved, but the approach to problem solving and the experience of utilizing others to help in problem solution can be carried over to the work or personal situation.

Career Advancement Problems

- I am unable to get from my manager good performance feedback on which to base a development plan. He/she keeps saying, "I'm doing just fine."
- I have little or no access to the informal social and political systems because I'm not invited to lunch, to play tennis, for a beer after work, etc.
- Jobs are filled before I find out they are open.
- My interest in and success at work is causing problems at home with a competitive spouse.
- I feel guilty about taking the time away from my children when I need to travel or work long hours. I have little energy when I get home at night.
- I feel strong conflicts about success in the corporation and maintaining my racial identity. Must I "become white" to succeed?

In dealing with development of solutions, workshop participants attack each problem with three questions in mind:

1. What must *I* do to improve this situation?
2. What must my *manager* (or spouse or son, etc.) do?
3. What can I do to *influence* my manager (or spouse or son, etc.)?

The approach is behavioral—not theoretical. For example, if home/

work conflicts are resulting in unmanageable time or emotional pressures, the team must come up with specific steps that can be taken. These might range from weighting a list of chores according to desirability and time and then having each spouse draw chores from a hat, to hiring a maid for five hours every other week. In addition, people are encouraged to determine whether the values and standards for roles and life style are their own or were simply picked up from parents or friends subconsciously. Once people determine their own values and priorities and act on them, they are less concerned with others' opinions and live to please themselves and significant others in their lives. They stop trying to please the world, and they minimize situations where guilt and anxiety are the outcomes. In problem solution, teams are encouraged to be as creative as possible and not to make value judgments. This allows people to test each solution on its own merits and pick and choose the ones they are most comfortable with.

In some cases, psychological issues are raised, such as maintaining racial identity, or dealing with personal feelings of femininity, or trying to decide where, if at all, one must personally compromise standards or preferences (e.g., language or dress). The trainer tries to guide the discussion to the question of conscious choice. Consequences of changing or not changing are explored in light of ultimate goals, and significant discussions result about such things as dress and how significant it really is (as opposed to being a symbol of independence). Again, the workshop leaders decline to make judgments about personal choices. They simply serve to help the thought process to a conclusion or point of decision for the participants involved.

Development of a Career Plan

One of the critical workshop objectives is development of a career plan. Participants reach far into the future to fantasize about the kinds of things they would like to do, achieve, possess, or have experienced in their lifetime; they then pull back to try to establish more specific, shorter-terms goals in support of those long-term goals. Broad life goals are set for such areas as learning, personal relationships, work, leisure, etc.; then a specific career plan is set in the context of those broader goals. If the participants lack the information to be very specific about career goals, they are encouraged to set some general career goals (e.g., a position of significant managerial responsibility within a large corporation) and then develop their action plan to get information they need to become more specific. For example, their plan might include setting up discussions with people in various parts of the company to find out what kinds of opportunities exist, or going to school to learn more about the technical aspects of a particular function. Exhibit C lists the type of approach used for establishment of life goals and career plans.

Summary

The Career Development Workshop is designed to help one focus on personal needs and priorities and to increase control of one's personal situation. It results in increased self-awareness and the improved self-confidence that comes with knowing and accepting one's strengths and limitations. In place with other programs it can be a positive approach to individual development, and organizations should consider it in their effort toward equal opportunity.

(Exhibits A, B and C are on the following pages).

CAREER DEVELOPMENT WORKSHOP AGENDA

I. *Introduction*. Presentation of workshop objectives and an opportunity for participants to get to know each other and to establish working teams.

II. *Who Has Control?* Using the film "You Pack Your Own Chute," team activities, and questions on control of one's life and work, personal concerns about change and taking risks are dealt with.

III. *Identification of Barriers to Success*. Teams identify barriers to personal achievement and analyze them. Particular attention will be given to problems related to being a woman or minority working in business today. Solutions to these problems will be dealt with throughout the session.

VI. *Who Am I?* Using a series of structured personal, team, and large-group activities, participants look at themselves in terms of strengths, areas needing improvement, past successes, likes and dislikes, and life roles.

V. *What Are My Work Values?* Participants examine conditions they like or don't like to work under and focus on what they are really working for.

VI. *What Are the Demands on Me?* Participants identify the roles they play and what specific behaviors are expected of them in these roles. Conflicting roles and demands are identified and solutions to role conflicts are examined in the group.

VII. *Where Am I Going and How Do I Get There?* Following review of the career development process, participants look at personal life and work objectives and begin to set goals.

VIII. *How Do I Overcome the Obstacles?* Teams work on practical solutions to problems identified in the workshop, and share and discuss them with the groups and the trainers in a nuts-and-bolts discussion.

IX. *Personal-Action Planning*. Individually, participants set specific six-month action plans, including steps to overcome problems.

TRAINER INSTRUCTIONS

Analysis of Strengths, Skills, Abilities, and Weaknesses (45 min.)

The purpose of this exercise is to take a broad look at each person's abilities and some of their limitations. Participants should be brainstorming to develop long lists of things about themselves (i.e., generating more self-inventory data).

Individual Activity (10 min.)

Have participants turn to the activities sheet. Read the instructions with them and give examples of your own strengths showing a very broad range of areas to draw upon (e.g., making people comfortable; solving complex mathematical problems; giving informal talks; water skiing; writing reports; following through on detail; etc.). People should include, but go beyond, work skills.

Encourage no limitations. Tell people to "blow their own horn." Put aside fears of being boastful, proud, ego-centered.

Have them be sure to turn the page and include weaknesses (only four or five). Tell them this should be easy to do! Once you feel people have exhausted their list, begin:

Team Activity (30 min.)

Suggest that people read their lists aloud slowly. After each person reads his or her list, have that person stop and let the group add things that they have observed so far.
People should feel free to add to their lists if someone else lists a skill or strength that they neglected. That is one of the objectives—to gain from each other.

Large Group Activity (5 min.)

In the large group, ask how people felt sharing these things. The feelings listed below should be included. If they don't come out in the group, add them and seek agreement.

1. It is easier to identify weaknesses and talk about them than strengths. We tend to think of ourselves in negative terms.

2. It is embarrassing to talk about one's strengths at first.

3. Once I am comfortable and know it's O.K. to talk about them, it feels good to say where I'm good.

Summarize that this is an additional group of data which we will be building on.

EXHIBIT C

LIFE AND CAREER GOALS

Exhibit C is so thorough and detailed that space does not allow more than a skeletal outline. Essentially, Exhibit C helps participants

- define a number of their long-term goals
- describe them in concrete terms
- weigh them for importance
- select the steps necessary to achieve them
- recognize obstacles to attaining the goals

- decide how to overcome the obstacles
- recognize who can assist in achieving the goals
- develop a method to measure and chart one's actual progress toward each specific goal

When Management Gets Involved: EEO at Citizens and Southern National Bank

Stanley M. Ginsberg

Citizens and Southern National Bank, one of Atlanta's largest commercial banks, recently embarked on a highly ambitious EEO program that could well serve as a model for other banks around the country. This is not a drastic change for C & S: Over the past ten years, its affirmative action plan has grown from a one-page hiring memo to a bound volume nearly five inches thick. In five years, the number of female employees in managerial and professional jobs has gone from 119 to 350; and the bank anticipates that within a year minorities will be at parity in official and managerial positions.

In the Beginning . . .

Citizens and Southern first began to look at its hiring patterns in the wake of the Civil Rights Act of 1964. Like most large businesses, it found imbalances in the number of women and minorities in the bank's work force. As a result, the director of personnel issued a one-page hiring memorandum urging that more women and minorities be brought into the bank, *primarily in clerical positions*. Although this still did not attack the root of EEO problems, it was an important first step.

Stanley M. Ginsberg is a New York City-based writer who covers business and management issues.

In mid-1973, top management began attending what has become an ongoing series of EEO meetings, seminars, and workshops. A strong commitment to affirmative action quickly took shape. Correcting numerical imbalances simply was not enough; in the words of Veronica Biggins, Citizens and Southern's equal opportunity officer:

> Our management doesn't simply consider EEO as something from the books. It's good business getting the best qualified people for our jobs. We are spending a lot of time with our top managers, getting the commitments that are needed. The problem is not with women and blacks in staff jobs, but with upward movement into higher-level managerial and professional jobs. Our emphasis now is on moving women and blacks into areas that traditionally have been white male. Our program is an aggressive one, but we still have a long way to go.

The bank's initial efforts at EEO were not without problems. At that time, all reporting involving employee data was done by hand, wasting time and energy that sould have been devoted to planning. For another thing, there was the economic slowdown. Faced with having to reduce staff, the bank chose to do it by natural attrition, rather than through layoffs and excessing; for over a year there was very little hiring of anyone, including minorities and women, thereby retarding the bank's original EEO timetable.

Early signs of recovery in 1975 allowed management to give more serious attention to affirmative action. As a first step, all personnel information was put into a computer system that reports not only numbers and percentages of female and minority employees, but departmental turnover, reasons for leaving, salary curves, and promotion/transfer patterns. In short, what took months of staff time before is now readily available as a printout, and planners can direct their attention to developing substantive programs. A second major development was the addition of a full-time equal opportunity officer responsible for coordinating line management goals with Personnel's staffing efforts aimed at filling both management and staff-level jobs. The Citizens and Southern Employee Relations Department involves nearly a dozen employees.

The Program

The C & S philosophy is that successful implementation of EEO planning depends upon the cooperation of line management. For this reason, divisional managers are brought into the planning process at the very beginning, and few planning decisions are made without their input.

At the earliest stages, line managers—working with the equal opportunity officer—analyze the EEO-1 Report for their areas of responsibility. For each department, questions need to be answered before yearly goals can be set:

- What growth is anticipated?
- What turnover is anticipated?
- What are the key jobs in the department—the jobs leading to officer level?
- What officer positions lead to higher positions?
- Where does underutilization still exist?

In addition, those areas or departments are identified that need special attention because of problems in achieving affirmative action goals. Accountability for failure to meet goals can be caused by failure of a manager to achieve his or her goals, or failure of employee relations to find candidates for openings.

Once the coming year's staffing needs have been determined and priorites established, the task of recruiting can begin. Here, too, line management plays an important role. Citizens and Southern has adopted a policy of promotion from within. Managers are expected to recommend promising employees from their own departments. Employee Relations posts all nonentry and nonofficer-level jobs and encourages employees to explore these opportunities. The bank's Training Department offers employees the chance to shape their future by developing other skills. The bank offers courses in commercial lending, collecting, and typing, among others. Says Ms. Biggins, "Training is good business—we're building and educating an internal manpower pool so that we can fill both present and future needs."

Outside recruiting presents its own problems. Atlanta, like many sunbelt cities, has become a highly competitive labor market. There is fierce competition for qualified employees not only with other banks, but also with brokerage houses and financial consulting firms. Consequently, Citizens and Southern has had to adopt an aggressive campus recruitment policy.

Recruiting for the bank's management training program is aimed at current employees, as well as qualified people outside the bank, primarily recent college graduates with business degrees. To attract the caliber of graduates it wants, the bank has found that a direct approach works best. Personnel recruiters work closely with deans and placement directors of colleges and universities with strong business programs. In addition to on-campus interviewing, the bank tries to reach qualified minority candidates through advertising in magazines and campus newspapers directed toward minority interests. The college program is not restricted to minority schools; Citizens and Southern also visits predominantly white schools, which are good sources of women and some black candidates, as well as of white males.

Ms. Biggins admits that one of the bank's biggest personnel headaches is the turnover of middle managers with two to five years' experience in the banking industry. Given the competitiveness of the Atlanta labor market and the relative scarcity of trained women and minority managers, this is not surprising: No sooner does a promising employee complete training than he or she is fair game for other industries.

As can be seen from the foregoing, the key to Citizens and Southern's AAP is involvement: Management at all levels is expected to take an active role in EEO planning, implementation, and review. In fact, so seriously does the bank view its commitment to affirmative action that a section on EEO performance has been incorporated into a new "management progress report," on which promotions and pay raises are based. Review of Citizens and Southern's affirmative action plan is the responsibility of the Affirmative Action Advisory Committee, whose membership roster reads like a profile of the Atlanta business community. Besides Citizens and Southern's president, Dick Kattel, and two General Vice Presidents, Bill Faulkner and Henry Collinsworth, there are also two women—Joan Crawford, manager of Lord & Taylor's Atlanta store, and Orinda Evans, a prominent attorney—and two blacks—Dr. Harding Young, a respected educator and member of the faculty of Georgia State University, and Lyndon Wade, director of the Atlanta Urban League. Both Ms. Crawford and Dr. Young are members of the bank's board of directors.

During the committee's reviews of the affirmative action plan, each department's goals are compared with actual progress. Corrective action or a change of emphasis may be recommended.

Cititzens and Southern tries to maintain an atmosphere of openness in its employee relations. Through the bank's grievance procedure, employees are encouraged to bring their dissatisfactions to the equal opportunity officer, who acts as an informal mediator. Managers are expected to participate in grievance discussions and take immediate corrective action on valid employee complaints. So far, Ms. Biggins reports, most disputes have been settled amicably, without recourse to outside agencies.

One often finds that a bank's planning and decision making originate at the top of the management pyramid, with little consultation at the middle management level. Progressive, far-reaching EEO programs are still very much in the minority. Citizens and Southern's commitment and record of success can well serve as a model, and as a fine example of what can happen when management at all levels gets involved.

International Paper Co. and the Middle-Aged Employee

Jacqueline A. Thompson

Of all the EEO legislation passed in the last decade, the Age Discrimination in Employment Act of 1967 (ADEA) is probably the most ignored and least enforced. Employment rights for the middle-aged is not the type of issue that captures EEO directors' attention or makes headlines. Furthermore, since ADEA has no affirmative action provision, it is easier for companies to ignore its basic intent, which is to promote the hiring of otherwise qualified older people (between forty and sixty-five years old) and to outlaw any arbitrary discrimination against that age group.

Because the law lacks teeth, most companies are only vaguely aware of its existence. An exception is the International Paper Company. International Paper is a world-wide land resource management company that, according to *Fortune* magazine, is the 52nd largest U.S. industrial corporation, with sales of over $3.5 billion last year.

One of International Paper's unusual features is the demographics of its employee population. A high proportion of its 52,287 employees are middle-aged, due to the company's low turnover rate and the fact that many of its plants and facilities are located in small, rural communities in the South.

Thus, regardless of ADEA, International Paper is one company that has not felt the need to change its hiring policies to attract older/ employees. In fact, if International Paper had a problem at all in the

Jacqueline A. Thompson, a New York City journalist, frequently writes on business and management issues.

area of middle-aged employment, it concerned quality, not quantity. Now, even that problem is well on its way to being solved.

The solution appeared in the unexpected guise of a management seminar. In early 1976, the company instituted a pilot program in one of its divisions to upgrade the management skills of its more senior supervisors and middle managers. The primary aim of the Experienced Managers' Seminar was to make supervisors in the Wood Products and Resources group aware of their responsibility for developing their subordinates, and a secondary aim was to improve their management style by uncovering and correcting any problems the seminar participants had in relating to other people. Indirectly, the program did much more. It remotivated and stimulated a group of over-40 employees, many of whom felt their potential for advancement had slowed to a standstill. These were employees who were still doing a good job for International Paper, but whose career prospects were dwindling compared to the average, young, professionally trained, college-educated forester on the way up.

"The seminar was surprisingly successful," says Carolyn Nauman, manager of personnel administration for Wood Products and Resources, one of International Paper's largest business groups (it encompasses one-quarter of the company's total professional and managerial population). The group is responsible for managing IP's 8.3 million acres of woodlands and for the manufacture of a variety of wood products, including lumber, plywood, and telephone poles.

Nauman explains that most of the seminar's 200 participants to date have been plant managers or area superintendents who supervise a group of foresters. Nauman says:

> Typically, the attendees are over forty, have no college degree, and have been with the company for years. Usually, they feel most comfortable outdoors and are unhappy behind a desk. Many have become frustrated and demoralized watching high-potential, young foresters rise quickly in the hierarchy when they perceive their own careers as dead-ended for all the wrong reasons.

According to Nauman, the course has had a startling effect on morale.

> To the participants, it was more than just an informative little seminar giving them feedback about how people perceive them and professional advice about team-building. The very existence of the course, to them, was concrete proof that the company had not forgotten them and did understand their needs. It was something positive being done to advance their careers.

233

Although it's still too early to assess the program's long-term impact, Nauman has detected some early signs of change. She claims that the graduates appear more goal-oriented and function more effectively as leaders. Moreover, they all seem confident that their superiors now recognize their contribution to the company's well-being and will act on the knowledge come promotion time. A few of the group, in fact, have already been promoted.

The program has now been expanded to include a new seminar called "Counseling on the Job." Both seminars are three to five days long and are conducted by a consulting psychologist at various training centers around the country.

Initially, managers were selected for the seminars by line officers or managers in charge of employee relations and management development. However, because of the program's enthusiastic reception, employees now ask to attend. In future, the program may be expanded to include all supervisors and middle-management personnel in the Wood Products and Resources group, no matter what their age.

Although the program has as yet received very little internal publicity, it has not gone unnoticed by International Paper's corporate-level human resources staff, particularly R. William Holland, who is manager of the company's affirmative action program. Holland functions as the company's EEO manager, responsible for rating the affirmative action efforts of all the business groups within IP. He has already commended the Wood Products group for its pioneering morale-building program and has indicated that the group can expect recognition on the company's affirmative action evaluation sheet at year's end.

At International Paper, the motivation and promotion of middle-aged managers is a measurable goal, for it has been incorporated into a unique, company-wide social accounting program. Under this program, such goals are termed "Budgeted Non-Financial Objectives," or BNFOs, a process adopted in 1974 as a way to focus management's attention on the company's more subtle problems in the areas of strategic planning, affirmative action, management and professional development, technology transfer, government affairs, and employee communication. The BNFO program is similar to "management by objectives" in that both provide a method for formulating goals and measuring achievement; BNFO is different in that it is intended to measure accomplishment solely in areas concerning highly visible public issues, areas that do not fit into the traditional business functions of finance, manufacturing, or marketing. The phrase "Budgeted Non-Financial Objectives" describes precisely what the goals entail. BNFO goals need not be measured in financial (or even quantifiable) terms. But they invariably require action in the social, technological, or governmental areas and must be incorporated into a company's short- and long-term planning and review process, i.e., be "budgeted," in order to be effective. In short, the BNFO process insures that a company's nonfinancial goals are as important as its financial ones, thus institutionalizing a new, nonmaterial value system within the organization.

The concept looks good on paper, but does it work? On the surface, BNFO sounds like just another management science gimmick, the construct of some publish-or-perish business school professor intent on devising a way to make corporations more respected by today's disenchanted public. However, at International Paper, the BNFO program has had a revolutionary impact for one very practical reason: senior managers' compensation is tied to their BNFO rating. A low rating translates into a smaller bonus.

Bill Holland can attest to the priority IP's senior executives now give to BNFO ratings since it is his job not only to help top management formulate affirmative action goals, but also to evaluate their performance come year's end.

"I can tell you one thing," says Holland, "BNFOs are taken very seriously at this company. Management really listens at mid-year when I sit down with them to discuss their progress and point out the ratings they are headed toward."

The establishment of the BNFO system is not the only proof of International Paper's good intentions in the EEO and employee development area. Two years ago the company was reorganized and the human resources department was expanded and radically upgraded. Today, more than one of IP's top officers has a personnel background.

Holland is an example of the kind of human resource talent the company has assembled. With a Ph.D. in political science from Michigan State, Holland left a teaching post at the University of California at Riverside to join IP. Holland says his underlying philosophy is that affirmative action means exactly that. It's an effort to focus on a problem or series of related problems in a positive, creative, imaginative way. He claims that the Wood Products and Resources program illustrates that approach.

On the surface, it appeared that there was very little to be done in an affirmative way for the over-40 manager. But that happened not to be true. Middle-aged managers are important to this company; they are long-service employees who are extremely knowledgeable about the business. By that fact they have an essential contribution to make. The Wood Products group had the foresight to identify some of these people, remotivate them, and use the talent that was lying dormant. In doing so, the group's officers had to take a close, critical look at how it was conducting its daily business. The group's profits will be affected positively by the program because an important group of employees is now working more productively. Happily, there is room in the BNFO process for Wood Products to get ample credit for its efforts.

Holland, who emphasizes that the Wood Products program may be complying with the spirit of ADEA, but that the letter of the law did not require it, perceives himself as a part of management and as concerned about profits as anyone else—hardly the attitude of the typical EEO officer.

Around here, human resources is well integrated into the company's line functions. After all, the variables that go into EEO decisions are very similar to those that go into profit-and-loss considerations. If I want a production person to be sophisticated about affirmative action, I have to be sophisticated about his production problems. I have to understand downtime and inventory buildups and safety requirements. If nothing else, it certainly facilitates communication—another of International Paper's BNFO goals.

A University Helps the Handicapped

Annette Power Johnson

Affirmative action for the handicapped has begun in both education and employment at Cleveland State University, Cleveland, Ohio. In 1973 university president Walter B. Waetjen appointed a committee on services to disabled students, with instructions to identify architectural, instructional, and procedural barriers to learning and to make recommendations to appropriate administrative officers. President Waetjen took this action six months prior to the signing of the Rehabilitation Act of 1973. In 1974, in light of Section 503 of the Act, he augmented the committee and charged it with developing affirmative action for employees. In addition, several academic departments and administrative units have been involved in programs related to disabled persons, programs which benefit university people as well as the greater community.

A survey of University buildings was done, and subsequent recommendations made, by disabled students who could readily assess the structures and interpret guidelines for building standards. These recommendations formed the basis for a proposal—submitted by the vice-president for campus planning, Thomas E. Haynes, and the chairperson of the president's committee on services to the disabled, Dr. Elsie M. Nicholson—to the Ohio Rehabilitation Services Commission for grant assistance, under the 1973 Act, to eliminate remaining architectural barriers at the university by year-end 1976. ORSC funded the University for $280,000, and the Ohio Board of Regents provided $70,000.

Annette Johnson is Affirmative Action Officer at Cleveland State University, Cleveland, Ohio.

Major architectural improvements (such as elevators, an entry ramp, and street modifications) will cost about $167,000. Other architectural modifications will cost about $140,000. Many learning center acquisitions will benefit the visually impaired: tape recorders, braille writers, porta-readers (which project material onto a screen), an optacon (which permits a blind person to read printed symbols through sensory transmission), raised-line drawing kits, an attachment enabling the university computer to produce braille material, etc. There will also be transportation and service facilities such as a specially equipped van for the disabled, a storage and service center for wheelchairs, and large brailled maps and signposts. We will have a lift unit to help people in and out of cars. The transportation center cost will be $18,000.

There are 155 disabled students enrolled for the 1975-76 academic year; of these, 59 receive direct services, an increase of 30 over the previous year. It is projected from public-school enrollments that by 1980 there will be 310 students requiring direct services.

The severely disabled persons hired in 1975-76 include two totally blind faculty members, a secretary using leg braces, two deaf custodial workers, and a visually impaired custodial worker. Services have been made available to these employees by many persons at the university. The Division of Special Studies has provided readers and support, departments have provided student assistants, Security has aided in emergencies, and employees and students have helped when needed. Considerable accommodations have been made for other employees with emerging disabilities.

Three custodial workers were recently hired after undergoing a twelve-week training course run jointly with Vocational Guidance and Rehabilitation Services, a private, nonprofit agency that has established training projects with several Cleveland area companies. The university provided training and equipment on campus; VGRS supplied the trainees and a counselor. A second group is now in training at the university. One person is a deaf mute, one has epilepsy, and one is visually impaired. Many of the trainees are from a minority group. The other custodial workers have been very cooperative, and many have had a trainee assigned to work with them.

The Division of Special Studies provides services and counseling for both students and employees. Activities have included selling tickets for wheelchair basketball games in the gymnasium, providing special parking spaces, scheduling readers, overcoming classroom obstacles, raising awareness and sensitivity, and making university programs—such as physical education and science laboratories—relevant to the disabled.

Two departments recently held a seminar, "Human Awareness and the Physically Disabled Student," in order to foster integration of physically disabled students into the mainstream of university life. A panel of both disabled and able-bodied students and employees discussed their personal reactions to their own or to others' disabilities. A blind student explained her reactions to the various types of assistance which have been offered her; a sighted student explained his feelings of uncertainty on how to relate to someone with a disability.

Cleveland State's social service department has a program in orientation and mobility instruction and is beginning a new program in rehabilitation of the blind. In these two programs are approximately thirty students, and three faculty members with degrees in several related areas. The speech pathology department operates a Speech, Language, and Hearing Clinic which offers help at nominal cost. Industry uses the clinic for testing purposes, and many CSU students are referred as a result of tests given entering students. The general public is charged on a sliding-scale basis so that no one will be turned away.

In cooperation with a local television station, ABC's WEWS, and on a grant from the Cleveland Foundation, Dr. Stanley Baran, a professor in the communication department, has been filming retarded youngsters in order to provide a constructive, healthy influence for them. He feels that television has a strong influence on many retarded people, and that it can be used to enhance their self-esteem and to provide positive models.

Cleveland State has one of the country's oldest cooperative education programs, in which students work outside the university in jobs related to their educational programs. Disabled students have always had access to the program, but employers are now much more receptive to hiring handicapped students. The cooperative education program is working with Dr. Elsie Nicholson, chairperson of the president's committee, to develop a work- and career-oriented experience for students with disabilities.

The physical therapy and occupational therapy programs have recently been recommended for accreditation. About sixty-five students are presently in the program. As part of their training they do field work in hospitals, community health facilities, and schools. Their six months of field work (three in psycho-social dysfunction and three in physical dysfunction) are done anywhere in the country. The elementary and special education department is working on many aspects of educating the handicapped. The federal government has mandated that schools use the least restrictive alternative in educating the handicapped, that is, that schools reduce as much as possible the segregation of the handicapped. The faculty are involved with local agencies in facilitating the mainstreaming of the mentally and physically disabled. The department's Special Services Center is used by 200 persons a week to improve their reading comprehension, eye development, vocabulary, and reading speed. Many of the clients are public-school students; some have significant learning disabilities.

As more handicapped individuals move into the mainstream of society in school and at work and become integrated, productive citizens, universities will be serving as resources for employers, educators, and public administrators. The universities will provide faculty and student specialists, educated handicapped employees, and—out of their own experience—assistance in making the changes required by law in education, employment, architecture, and transportation.

DEC